PLANTAINS
AND
OUR BECOMING

PLANTAINS
AND
OUR BECOMING

MELANIA LUISA MARTE

Tiny Reparations Books

An imprint of Penguin Random House LLC
penguinrandomhouse.com

LIBRARY OF CONGRESS CATALOGING-IN-PUBLICATION DATA

Names: Marte, Melania Luisa, author.
Title: Plantains & our becoming / Melania Luisa Marte.
Other titles: Plantains and our becoming
Description: [New York] : Tiny Reparations Books, [2023]
Identifiers: LCCN 2022055578 (print) | LCCN 2022055579 (ebook) |
ISBN 9780593471340 (paperback) | ISBN 9780593471357 (ebook)
Subjects: LCGFT: Poetry.
Classification: LCC PS3613.A77763 P57 2023 (print) | LCC PS3613.A77763 (ebook) |
DDC 811/.6—dc23/eng/20221216
LC record available at https://lccn.loc.gov/2022055578
LC ebook record available at https://lccn.loc.gov/2022055579

Printed in the United States of America
1st Printing

Interior art: Leaves © Yuliia Khvyshchuk / Shutterstock.com

BOOK DESIGN BY KRISTIN DEL ROSARIO

For all lovers born the color of earth.
This book is for us.

CONTENTS

PART ONE

DAUGHTER
OF
DIASPORA

Afro-Latina

According to *Merriam-Webster*, the term *Latina* was invented in the 1970s to describe a woman who is a native inhabitant of Latin America living in Latin America or the United States. *Merriam-Webster*, however, does not consider *Afro-Latina* a word. In America's most trusted dictionary, Latin American people of African ancestry do not exist. It is an unofficial term attributed to those who have felt the noose but have only loosely been hung by the tree. Or maybe she is the tree? The way her roots always got they foot on the neck of all cultures. Thank a Black woman for always giving you something to be microaggressive about. To fawn over in disbelief.

Latina, an adjective that behooves to be seen. *Afro-Latina*: a myth. A folk tale. A thing she becomes after the search party leaves. Like she hadn't been standing there all along. Clearing the forest, while you grind her bones to fertilize the soil. This isn't a metaphor for *Black-girl-magic* or anger. This is me, no longer flat ironing my 'fro to fit inside a term dependent on my proximity to whiteness.

I am not Black and Latina. I am a Black Latina. I am an anomaly strangers whisper about, confident my tongue don't conjugate like theirs. I am creating my own eulogy before they write me out of the wrong story. Contort my surviving into their savior. Build me a shrine to die on. Haven't we always been damaged goods? Sold at a bargain price. Carbon-copy us into ash. Snap their fingers and blow us into dust. Her silhouette, the standard. Her Afro, a wig they take on and off. Her melanin packaged and sold. Her culture, a billion-dollar commodity. *Merengue. Bachata. Salsa. Dembow. Reggaeton. Palo. Rumba. Samba. Tango.* Name a beat her hips ain't formed. And twerked into *baile*. Into *ritmo*. Into *música*. When Celia says, *La Negra tiene tumbao*, she is speaking for millions of Afro-Latinas who go missing in history books. On television. In movies. In conversations about their own identities. In real life. Afro-Latinas. Black women. Poor women. Marginalized women. Are targets. Are dying. And those who love her culture won't attend her funeral. Will not speak of her life. Instead tape up her house. Ready to thrift and shop her culture away. Buy up heirlooms and call them spicy. Bloody red with passion. Do you see it? How easily Black girl becomes wallpaper to the building of her own identity. A mime always in front of her to edifice a movement.

My culture is not your cash crop.
My mother's country is not your paradise.
My bilingual tongue is not your inquisition to crusade over.

Dicen que *"soy Latina,"* until I start talking about colorism.
Until I check them on erasure.
Until I choose to speak on my own behalf.
Until I remind them my Afro comes before Latina.

Volvio Juanita /
La Maleta

Mami & Papi
carried   more
than   clothes
back to the States. Mami lost her tan. Papi lost his patience.
Mami packed a mystified mirror of nationalism. Papi packed
hair grease, an Afro pick, and a Presidente. Mami forgot if she
was ever really Black since she was taught to be everything and
nothing. Mami, daughter of Juanita, was born with kinky hair
and confused roots and *maybe* ignorance became her bliss and
beauty as much as it became her birthright. She packed hair
relaxer, *rolos*, and cigarettes. Papi never got to tell us how he
made peace with his dark skin. His skin made white women
clutch their purses. His skin got him arrested at customs for hu-
man trafficking. His skin—the type that got you calling your
light-skin mama to hire lawyers and pay bail. His skin got
people making all types of assumptions. Skin that made cops
ask for papers and receipts. Skin. All it takes is a particular
shade of skin. Skin that left Mami with 3 unambiguously
Black babies and stares. Skin that let them know exactly what
Papi looked like. Casket fresh & Black. Skin that called us *Ne-
gro*, *Prieto*, *Moreno*, *Africano*. Anything but *Blanco*, *fino*, *pelo
bueno*. I once heard someone in my family call us *indiecito* and
I laughed. You mean, Indigenous as in African? As in,

the Blacker the berry, the harder it is for you
to loosen the noose.

What Are You
Mixed With?

—Arranged marriages and feminine virginity.
—Telemundo and BET.
—Beyoncé and Fefita la Grande.
—Mangoes and plantains.
—Hammocks and daily naps.
—Coconut oil and olive oil.
—The exploitation of my father's strength.
—The fetishizing of my mother's beauty.
—A *palo* dance circle in a *batey* and a swag surf in the club.
—Caribbean spice and Southern BBQ.
—Humorous Black Twitter and sad-girl memes.
—Yo' mama jokes and afterschool cyphers.
—The trauma of Trujillo and the hope of Obama.
—A New York City summer and a Dominican winter.
—The exhaustion and excitement of having to answer
A question that seems as foreign as you.

Smuggling A Mango
Is Hard

Origin: The mango is native to southern Asia. It spread early on to Malaysia, eastern Asia and eastern Africa. Spanish and Portuguese explorers of the fifteenth century brought mangoes to the Caribbean along with genocide, slavery and whitewashed religion.

I tried smuggling a mango through customs. I got caught and pulled to the side. They asked if there was anything in my bag that could be incriminating. I confessed; *I've got three mangoes from my grandmother's garden.* He opens my bag and confiscates them, leaves the bottle of foreign liquor and winks at me. I don't tell him that the mango is more valuable than the liquor. I don't tell him that this mango has helped nourish a home out of many shamed bodies, a dysmorphia of scattered features. That America has waged a war on anything foreign, including organic fruits, cultures and people. I don't tell him that he is building a wall on my childhood and that this is a souvenir from a tiny paradise. I don't tell him that I wonder if he would be giving me such a hard time had I been a white tourist co-opting "tropical vibes" for the aesthetic of erasing Indigenous cultures and people.

Right before stealing my mangoes, this white Latinx man proceeds to say, *"Pero eres una morena bella y que tu eres?"* Which translates to, *You are such a pretty Black girl, what are you?* I chuckle or choke. Finding it not-so-funny how anti-Blackness translates so well. His question posing between bleach and sun. A fetishized love trial. My genetic makeup, a lab experiment. How even the language of romance has a fear of Black beauty. How startling of me to be pretty for a Black girl in two separate languages. Assimilate to these constructs of beauty and still be seen as collateral damage. Me, market-fresh produce waiting to be spritzed and labeled. Appraised at a boosted bill for the joy of stuffing me into two different boxes. Both Black and foreign. Both Black and woman. All foreign and Black and woman. How the prickling of my skin fumigates his slander, pulpifying my pride back into its fruit.

There is not enough juice in me today to come up out this pacified demeanor. Not enough code-switching to stitch me back together. I smile, all nervous, all shaken, still unbothered with white probing, all light-skinned and some privilege. Still tired. Still zesty and firm, denying another man agency to comment on my body. Reminded that I am always the question mark at the end of *What are you mixed with?* I reply, *Have you ever tried chewing on a mango seed?* Don't.

Island Gyal

before the girliesss tussle 'bout it
remember that manhattan is an island too
i was raised in loisaida, the lowa, baruch projects
the crevice between the fdr drive & the ave
i wasn't born an island gyal
but the vibes suit me
ni de aquí ni de allá is a farce
and i would like to move past the fallacy
of claiming nothing when you're made of everything
some women have labored in boats
some babies are born over ocean water
some of us have wasted too much time wading
in water instead of living and winning
this is the poem that dances with both hips
this is not to discredit the confusion or pain
this is just a reminder that all energy has purpose
and wouldn't you rather spend it whining that waist
and touching the earth than explaining
to some uncultured fool how you,
poor you, blessed and favored you,
were gifted too much culture
and too much light
and too much talent
and too much body
and too much history
and too much autonomy
and you foolishly have no idea what to do with it.

Swallowing Teeth

- The first time it happened I was five. A baby tooth that got punched in by my oldest brother. It slid pass my tongue and clung to my throat. I swallowed in horror. He laughed with honor. He thought himself heroic and mighty. I learned fear before I learned words. He says it was already unhinged and he, gentle boy, tried to be helpful. I hadn't yet mastered ducking and he hadn't learned the word *femicide* yet. The way it forces a fist in your mouth leaves the shape of a woman trapped on an underground train looking for an exit begging to find her next breath.

- The second time I was seven and Lloyd pushed me dramatically to the ground. I was devastated. My crush on him would have to fade for he was a boy with an anger problem and thought little girls in overalls were worthy stepping-stones. I counted my scrapes and stopped daydreaming about Lloyd and tulips. I built a barbed wire fence around my skin, called it a garden and buried what was left of my baby teeth within the soil.

- The third time I was ten and breathless. My fifth-grade teacher, whom I liked, broke my heart. More than broke, left me feeling less human and more monster. She called me *mean* and *bossy* so I learned to shrink. I hunched more. I spoke less and listened obediently. I developed scoliosis and anxiety. I developed imposter syndrome and a tiny white woman inside my head who was always telling me what a mean and bossy, unloved little girl I was. She smiled at her achievement, receiving a teacher-of-the-year trophy. I smiled at her entitlement. I learned that monsters are good at teaching others to swallow teeth for fear they might never find the strength to uncover their own.

- The fourth time I was twelve and Jacob with a hairy unibrow said my arms looked like Chewbacca's. I said right back atcha. But I went home and cut off skin in an attempt to shave off the hair clinging to my arms. The meat of the cut trampolined up and the scar would not fade. My forever insecurity blanket. This time I swallowed more than just teeth; the blood made its way down my throat just as easily.

- I decided once the baby teeth were gone, I would stop dying a little each time someone asked me to swallow their disdain, their fears, their reflections. There was nothing left to swallow but my own truth. Instead, I learned to sharpen my fangs, I learned to chew my food nice and slow. Swallowing teeth taught me to spit up all my inhibitions and give birth to all the versions of me begging to be freed.

Coming To America
In III Parts

I. The year is 1963 and Rafael Trujillo, a gruesome dictator in the Dominican Republic, has been dead for 2 years. The government is unstable and the United States has offered visas to those who can afford it. My grandmother has six kids and three baby daddies, she's ready to leave this country and her triflin' ex-husbands behind. She buys her way out of the country and settles in the promised land. Señora Luisa exhausted all the teachings of ladyhood and societal clout as the daughter of a Dominican politician in Santiago to prove herself worthy of a green card. Before her Prince Charming came along, she spent her days sewing up a blanket of dreams. Needling through years' worth of fabric to afford her children's residency in America. Coming to America affords you the luxury of making a little less for the promise that one day your kids will make a little more. Isn't the American dream so ridiculous and enticing?

II. My father, a newfound American citizen, arranges to marry a woman he has only met on the phone, thus becoming my mother's ticket out of a poor Dominican ghetto. This being what the '90s taught me about how beauty and virginity were exchanged for passport stamps or the Dominican virgin rendition of *Pretty Woman*. My mother is 21, an unplucked flower desperate to see more than the garden she has grown too big for. My great-aunt has convinced herself she is a botanist matchmaker determined to pair an orchid with a black rose. And maybe even have their first sprout named after her. My father, smitten with the idea of being the first to pluck this orchid, travels through fields to reach her. *Notice how much we are conditioned as women to use*

our bodies and beauty to survive? There is nothing foreign about this
cycle of romantic entrapment.

III. My coming to America: how a first-generation American learned the
ropes to dodging the hard questions like *Where are you from?* and
How are you Black but speak Spanish? whilst seemingly having blue
passport privilege all the while growing up in the projects of New
York City. I don't know much about struggle, is what I have con-
cluded. I do know I have yet to see a crystal stair. It's been tight walk-
ups ten flights above and the elevator, always broken or unhinged. My
mama and neighbors' tempers and paychecks hanging by a loose
thread. The baby bloods threatening me with a butter knife. They
called us underprivileged or underserved. Either way, we so invisible
in this city. It's been hot sweaty train rides to the Bronx and back. It's
been summer flights to visit family living in wooden cabins. It's been
amoeba pains from drinking unfiltered river water. It's been poor but
at least we hoodrich. It's been the best time of my life during the worst
of circumstances and conditions. *I have nothing but grace and glory for
the tiny hoods and barrios that raised me.*

A Newlywed American Portrait:
My Mother & Father
Handcuffed At Customs

i picture them so innocent and young. maybe they wore white linen as new-lyweds often do. outfits coordinated and tailored. the air on the plane from haiti to florida smelling like vanilla cake and champagne. the flight atten-dant is singing, "*por que dios te hizo tan bella*." i picture them dancing salsa as they land in miami. the humidity, their hips swinging. security already warned, keep an eye on them. they must've seemed too joyous and carefree. too busy smiling and dancing onto the promised land. i picture my mother six months pregnant with my oldest brother. my father, a nervous happy wreck. my mother, angry that he claimed her as his own. my mother, insist-ing she does not know this man. my mother, hoping he makes it out free so he can send help. my father, reaching for his new wife. my mother, calm and calculated. my father, pulling out his blue passport as if it were a trophy. my father and his trophy wife are being detained. my mother, knowing they know her documents are fake. my mother and father handcuffed at cus-toms. my father, fitting the description of *el machete*, the lawyer he paid off who made immigration easy for so many. with his help, you no longer needed to climb a border or survive a boat ride. with his help, you could make it to the states in a first-class seat. with help, reparations came faster for *caribeños*. with access, thousands of families got to eat good, not just enough. the truth is, i come from immigrants who came from immigrants who came from stolen people who learned to survive on land they did not steal nor did they inherit. they simply squatted and plotted and peeled themselves a meal, an acre, a home. i come from loopholes and grievances and immi-gration lawyers who get paid to turn a criminal into an exceptional negro. i come from detention centers, and green land, and busy saintly streets. and maybe this is not my land but who is more deserving of it than me?

What Is Missed

When you leave the only home you have ever known
Even the bad things start to be missed. Something that
Used to be a pest can somehow feel like a gift. *You never
know what you're gonna miss,* Mami and Papi would say.

Papi missed salsa dancing and fresh cold beers on Sunday
nights in *La Zona Colonial*, the camaraderie of mechanic
friends who celebrate a long day with a meal of *chuleta
& mangú*, the dominoes gambling in front of the
     colmadón.

Mami missed cooking stews over rocks and burnt wood
at her local river, the scent of Abuela's dragon tree, the smell
of *jabón de cuaba* and the white noise of bucket showers.

You never know what you're gonna miss but when home
Becomes a hole from which you can never climb out of.
     A place
You have outgrown. When you can't afford basic human
     rights
Then you must leave home that very night. You must spend
The last of your savings and buy a flight, a bus, a seat on
     a boat.
You must map out your goal, your wishes, a five-year plan.
Think about the new home and its smell, the colors,
The furniture, will there be grass and a backyard?

You must pack a small suitcase and not look back.
Looking back will hurt. It will hurt more than staying.
And you can't afford to hurt when you can't even afford
To eat. And home is nothing without a kitchen and money
For food. They say home is where the heart is. I was taught
Otherwise. Home is where the stomach is safe, loved,
Unafraid that the next meal will come.
When you no longer eat with knots of insecurity. Home is a
    security blanket. Home.
How do you know when you have it? Easy. If you have
    to ask . . .
You do.

Mami & Technology

My mother loves technology. Loves Xoom and WhatsApp.
How she can transfer money to her mother with
A swipe of a finger. The app will even deliver the money to
Abuelita's door in cash and with the currency converted.
My mother loves the faces my grandmother makes when
She discovers something new on her iPhone. The way
It can take many different shapes. From telephone
To calculator to video camera to teleporting you
To your daughter. Can make you feel like years
Haven't gone by without kissing her face, or rubbing
Her back or seeing her smile. You see, before iPhones
And WhatsApp, my mother loved calling cards. Loved
the way she could send her family kisses through the phone
And remember the reason she left her homeland.
For progress and resources. It gives her pride to know
That they didn't resent her for leaving and having to
Wait years before she could return.

My mother loved keeping a calling card in her purse for
When her heart ached with familiar but distant hugs
    and voices.
She'd send me to the grocery store to fill her inventory
of missing ingredients: *milk, cereal, Goya beans and rice*
    for dinner. And don't forget a ripe avocado and a
    sweet plantain for frying.
Don't forget the adobo and a pack of sopitas,
Grab some red onions and a bunch of fresh cilantro.

And lastly, calling cards from the bodega right down
  the block.
The one that has the calling cards she loves the most.
She says they don't do her dirty and steal her minutes.
They actually give her a full 60 minutes for five dollars
Of her hard-earned money cleaning offices.

Mami loves technology for the same reasons
She loves to call herself a resident and not a citizen
She wants to remember the staying more than the leaving.

Immigrant
Math Problem

If I give Mamá 5,000 pesos and Mamá gives 3,000 pesos to Tío for groceries and gas.

And Tío gives 1,000 pesos to *la colmadera* for food, 500 pesos to *el pompiador* for gas and 500 pesos to his son.

And *la colmadera* gives 200 pesos to her daughter for *motoconcho* fare to ride to school.

And *el pompiador* gives 300 pesos to his wife for breakfast and dinner ingredients.

And Mamá leaves 2,000 pesos for a small emergency. And keeps X amount of pesos in some nook and cranny that she calls a bank. And the bank is her home because she says the real bank that's owned by the government is unsafe. And at least in her home she keeps the money buried right next to her loaded gun.

And
And
And how much more money do you think we will collectively need to erase the centuries of disenfranchisement that plagues us?

Mami and Mamá have always taught me money is like a waterfall for people like us. It must trickle down or else some of us will drown of thirst. I want a math problem that will teach me to make enough to save us all.

Abuelita's Garden

Dios te me bendiga are her first words to her garden. Early mornings, after the roosters are done preaching and the dogs have stretched downward and long. Their spines, a half moon of fur and muscle. The birds chirp in search of crumbs and water. Pebbling through air and ground, they find Abuelita's basket of scraps left out for them to feed. In her garden, there is always something for someone to feed. No thing is left homeless.

Dios te me bendiga, she glides through her garden. Broom in hand, a thing hugging leaves and slim branches. An upended bouquet of shrub—greenery embracing a saged wooden pole. Everything about this woman could decompose and leave not a site of ruin. I admire that. How much of this earth she honors and will one day become. There is a lesson in humility only those who have seen the bottom of an empty stomach can fathom. There is a lesson in survival only those who have seen the earth turn over and spill its fruits can witness.

Mouth dry and aching, many have found solace in my abuelita's garden. A water apple, a warm cup of coffee, a sweet soursop, green bananas, a buttery avocado, an earthy cup of dragon tea. The world's best mangoes. Her garden is a multivitamin, breakfast or dinner. Each disciple, lucky for the harvesting season. My abuelita, the apothecary, the *curandera*, the cook.

Dios te me bendiga, after the wilderness is done rejoicing, it's her time to speak of God and miracles. Her plants dewy and grateful. Here is a mother who loves them as if they were birthed from her womb. And just as wise as the earth they rose from. Abuela affirms them before the sun affirms more.

Dios te me bendiga, mi negra bella, mi poeta, mi semilla, mi bendecida. Her blessings are a garden of endless love. They tell me live, live because you sprung from me. Live because I dare you to. Live and thrive. Thrive because the birds, the flowers, the reptiles, we all want to witness your glory. Abuelita's garden is my favorite reminder that you don't need to be one specific kind of magical to bloom.

We are all becoming our best greenest thing. We slouch and freeze, we stunt and cry. We look up and there is a star warming our skin. There is a hand blessing our flesh. From dust to depression, we become. From twirls and teachings, we rejoice. *Dios te me bendiga*, and we all bloom.

Telling Time

I am (4)

My mother is packing two bags and dragging three kids. The cab she called is downstairs. She is trembling and I am crying. I tell her I want to stay with Papi. But she has decided to leave him and his fists back home. She tells me, *Time will tell you the truth about your father.*

I am (5)

My mother sneaking a cigarette in the restroom nervously picking at her chapped lips. She has not been very loving to herself today. Her skin is pleading for water. But there is a drought in her mind. Her new man goes to make love to his ex-wife.

I am (6)

My mother is crying into her phone yelling *please don't go* to a man I'm not sure she is even truly in love with. Somehow, she has convinced herself she needs him. That same night she threatens to take pills at the thought of living without him. He stays. A part of the woman I thought she was leaves.

I am (8)

and fatherless, or fathergone or fatherdead, searching for the 200-pound teddy bear that used to take me and my brothers to McDonald's on weekends. Every now and then I remember his funeral and cry in confusion. In retaliation I throw away the pink jewelry box with a heart-shaped clock he gifted me. I say, *What's the use of telling time, if it means you run out?*

I am (10)

and afraid that this body will never morph into something pretty enough to be saved. You know, like the fairy tales. Like my favorite princess cassette. Like the Spice Girls when they sang, *If you wanna be my lover.* Like when my mother pushes me to be super-smart, convinced I can't survive off beauty as she has done.

I am (12)

and wishing to die, telling my body that if it truly wanted us to live, it would lose thirty pounds and brain cells before the start of ninth grade. When begging didn't work. The depression and fat shaming continued. I thought I would never make it to graduation. I counted the days and hours until my emancipation from the public school system and the bullies who poked fun at their own poor misshapen mirrors.

I am (15)

and afraid that I've grown too big for my own skin. Everything about my existence feels wrong and untimely. I want to die but instead I write. Time follows me.

I am (18)

and anemic. The weight is finally off but I still don't feel pretty enough for this world. I give up and decide to be brilliant instead. I decide I will be a famous writer someday, and I jot down story ideas and poems in between breaks as a cashier at Fine Fare. Working a dead-end job is fundamental to the authenticity of this timeproof experience.

I am (21)

My mother has healed her anxiety but is triggered when she sees the signs in me. A water fountain of insecurities, tearing into oblivion. She begins to feel as if time has betrayed us both.

I am (26)

and finally feel like I love myself. Enough to say yes to living a grand life I am proud of. I move to the island that makes me feel my freest and I marry the man who feeds me mangoes. I shower myself in flowers of self-care and get paid to write the stories that make me dream. Time no longer feels like my enemy. Time has become my friend.

I am (28)

finally having morphed into ice cream worth scooping. People applaud when I speak, or breathe, or smile. I finally know how to tell time and let time tell me everything I want to hear: *You will bend time. Time will be your only true friend. Tell time what you want and time will deliver. Time will tell you the truth about your destiny. Trust in the timing of you.*

Serpentine Salon

It isn't wrong to be both brown-skinned and tender-headed.
After years of perm, roll, heat, and blowouts
from before you began to hemorrhage and scissor dance.
Every period and blowout a bloody reminder,
in this present we pay to hurt, in this past we were born
    to die.
In some future we are whole and complete.
No sweat-swaddled salon or standard stoop to slowly
    condense from.
Heaven be reincarnating: first unloved, now tree-hugging
    crop.

It isn't wrong to be both snake and strange fruit.
Your wrath for the wretched plague of wicked humans.
You decide to be reptilian if you cannot be perfection.
This is just a cry for help, when you scrape your scalp anew.
Your mother fainting at the sight of two decades of privilege
building in your tight curls . . .

She screams, Why didn't you just build yourself a rope?
That hair was strong enough to entice any American man.
One who could see you as more than just an immigrant
    child,
a spicy dream, a loud mouth with long teeth and fur.
You could've climbed so much higher with that hair.
I raised you better which means I raised you proper,

not with pearls and seething corsets but with slick sense
to manipulate men into exchanging their dollars for
your honey-colored eyes and softened mane.
I raised you better, not bitter.
Not heavy with negro-pessimism and slain remorse.
Have you no idea what your beauty has cost me?
And because I want more for you, I gave you my all.
What an ungrateful child, what women would pay for
    that hair.

It isn't wrong to crave beauty beyond
the color of bleached skin & burnt kinks.
You have been growing past your mother's wishes
long before that perm made you find God.
Long before that boy called you *big nose* and *fat back*.
Long before the grief of beauty made you drop-dead
    gorgeous.

Way back when, you, a small mermaid rising black & blue
    from tortured sea.
You say you wanted to touch your scalp and wet soil.
You say the beach was no place for cowardly lies.
You say you want to confront your mirror,
been wasting behind this brown paper bag far too long.
You say you want to be a fire, an avalanche, a bomb,
anything but docile, anything but a passing wave
that loses its power against white bodies.
Something that unfurls with claws and fangs,
a venomous thing. Greasy and hairless.
Coiling tightly, embracing the bite and taste of white meat.
Swallowing its last supper. All suffering
deeply buried in the belly of this massive beast.

It isn't wrong to fireball into something that dies with a
    vengeance,
that no longer cries or begs or shortfalls just to be praised.
No mausoleum or coaxing your body, you will never come
    back the same.
After what they have done to you, they'll call you villain.
    We see our hero.

Telenovelas /
How I Learned To Be A Girl

Ven, she'd say, *que tengo que peinarte esa melena.*
Oh, how I loved sitting between her thighs while she
greased my scalp, twisted this mane, and I could talk about
all the things only women like my mother had answers to.

Yet here, there is a moment of every brown and black girl's
childhood where she begins to question if she exists.

We sit in front of TV screens on couches, floor pillows,
in wooden *mecedoras*. Our mamas, grandmamas, *tías*
unbinding our hair, combing through knots. The telenovela
plays in the background. Except we become the background.

The painting on the wall of the house of the main character.
We, a tiny speck of brown. Like sand, we slip through
    stereotypes,
the boxes we climb out of. Still feeling so tiny and
    insignificant.
The cleaning lady, the enslaved mistress, the one *negra* in a
    crowd.

They don't even try to figure us out or fix their screen or go
to therapy and explain their disdain. There is no longer
an imagined reality where we can excuse this kind of
    violence.

This is how we come to terms with a world that belittles all
that we are in hopes of assimilation.
We, hungry for home, buy into whatever they're selling.
To maybe one day feel worthy of starring in our own
	telenovela.
To have a stage all to herself, one where she can dream of a
	world
that won't swallow her for being born the color of earth.

This is how we learn to mourn all that we will never be,
so we can celebrate and love   all that we are.

Good Evening, Officer

Non-melanated police officer pulls me over. I check my meter. At the time, I may have been going exactly 35 miles per hour. My mother taught me to be precise in that way. I roll down my window. Relieved I look cute today. My contour looks flawless. My highlighter is beaming. I've got the perfect pair of earrings on. They are giving off "harmless chick who is willing to use her everything to crawl herself out of this white man's overuse of power" fashion vibes. I happen to be wearing a black turtleneck. I begin to question my choice of outfit. Was this the reason he stopped me? Has he been warned that the people are reawakening? That they are no longer sleeping? Has he been warned that exuding unfiltered joy is also an act of political warfare? That my resistance is in the subtle way I smile at him? All proper and well-fed. Being soft and stern has its perks. There's something so powerful about sharing your magic but suiting up when someone wants to outright steal it. And we women are very intuitive in this way. I am trying not to be so analytical about my own choice of clothing. So I tell myself, *He seems well-versed on the nuances of urban thotties.* He's a young cop from the South and I'm sure he has Instagram and is up to speed that this is the kind of outfit an artsy ho would wear, anyways, because aesthetics. Also, I'm from New York and people from New York are just naturally interesting so I contemplate that maybe he stopped me to compliment me on how interesting I look. But probably not. So I roll down my window. I say, *Good evening, officer.* He smiles and says, *I'm going to need to see your license and insurance.* I ask him if I did something wrong other than the obvious things that could be wrong about this particular situation for someone like me in a country like this. He tells me that I was driving 5 miles above the speed limit. I apologize. Tell him I thought I was driving slow but I must've been mistaken. I apologize once more. The "sorry" echoes out of me like I am pleading for my life. To be spared another day. To let me choose how I wish to die. He looks at me, in such a way. As if to say, *How dare you?* Be Black and a woman and pretty and happy? Daughter of immigrants whose native tongue I use at my convenience. How dare I? Live the joyous life my grandmothers prayed for. Have the audacity to claim America as my own. How dare I claim a country that doesn't love me as my own? I smile at him, in such a way. As if to say, *How dare you? Do you not realize? That anything you can do, I do in heels all the while bleeding?*

On Voting

things i knew about adulting: grown folks had sex and grown folks had the right to vote. and i couldn't wait to be an adult so i could finally have a seat at the political table. i lost my virginity to obama. as in, i got to vote for the change i thought i was going to see in the world. and then i got to vote again. and then i voted for the white woman who may or may not actually believe my life truly matters, whose husband called people like us superpredators, and whose very grimace let you know that this was an acceptable white woman but not a morally kind one. and then i had to face some hard realities that i was voting alone and that the white feminists were not gonna come save me and maybe they wanted people like me dead. or gone. gone because who would think to vote for a demented 'phobe who hates everyone but himself and maybe even himself because have you seen his makeup? and now i think back on how my mother has still yet to become a citizen of these united states and has essentially lived/paid taxes for more than 30 years and has never had the right to vote. and is the right to vote that important if her life is just as it is whether she voted for that white man or the other white man or the biracial man who is visibly black but not too black that he would remind folks of mlk. and if you do happen to look like mlk what luxuries of running for president are not afforded to you and how do i raise a child to believe they can one day be president if i'm not even sure this country will not make his life harder than it needs to be because of something as small as skin gradation and what do i do with all my pessimism because y'all talkin' 'bout voting and i'm still stuck on how to make it through a year that feels like every horrid election year rolled into one. and if they do make it that far, what dehumanizing compromises will they have to make to get to be the face of small progress. and for those who do not have a head start by either race or class or by gender, how do they make it to the promised land? and then i go back to being born on election day in 1993 and how the bronx was on fire and my mama was glad this would be her last birth because this was intense and the hospital was in uproar because giuliani won and i was born with gray hair and i'm like, the way my anxiety been set up since day one, this all makes sense. and my brother text me: "have you filled out your absentee ballot?" to vote for a president i do not want and cast a vote in a red state i do not love to continue participating in a democracy that had to be forced to allow me to vote in the first place for people that do not care if i live or die because it turns out we may have been better off segregated than whatever "fake equality" this country pretends to be. and somehow at 26 i am back at the same chaotic hospital i was born at to continue reliving the same tired nightmare in the hopes that, one day, the maze will drop me off at a country who does not use my blood to oil its machine.

On The Subject
Of Cardi B

Imagine all the dissertations they'll write about her, hood girl anomaly.
She break English into hungry mouths and swollen bellies.
She speak like she eat *plátanos fritos* and fried chicken.
She be culture and language and seasoning.
The hot iron seething in our throats.
Saliva boiled over Ebonics simmers into an American canon.
The code switch tick over Belcalis and Beethoven.

On the subject of Belcalis Almánzar.
Of holding on to your birth name so the world won't butcher it.
On the subject of navigating patriarchy and politics in a time of
    reinvention
and simultaneous praise and rejection.

On the subject of Cardi B: half woman, half God.
Nonhuman thing. Stripper royalty turned feminist hood rap icon.
A Bronx queen who turned a stripper pole into a throne.

Hood girl anomaly seen as abstract.
#HoodGirlMagic and excellence always seen as abstract.
They always want to copy but never give credit.
Hood girls keep the cultural world afloat and never
even get a thank-you or proper respect & praise.
On the subject of hood girl magic and excellence always
appropriated and commercialized but still seen as abstract.

On the subject of bad bitches choosing themselves,
carving floral crowns out of concrete.
Painting them red with the blood of their haters,
dropping low so you can catch all these angles . . . Okurrrrrr.

On the subject of savior and self-worship and self-sufficiency
    and Cardi B
Hood Rat Aphrodite with *sazón* on her lips and a sniper for a mouth.

Cardi says everybody always got an opinion about her
and how she pop her kitty. Who she doin' it for?
Why she so proud of her small world built into empire?

Why she so happy and unashamed?
Why she gotta dress like that?
Why every word coming out her mouth
got third world poverty and first world vanity?
How dare she have expensive taste and
a bank account to match.
How dare she break her own ceiling?
How dare she reach for the stars?
How dare they gift her a high-fashion space suit,
televise her landing, watch her twerk as she plants
her hood rat flag on the moon and sings . . .
Honestly, don't give a f*ck bout who ain't fond of me
Because respectability politics are canceled.

Hood Galore

I learned opulence from Mami.
Even though she knew nothing of old money
She got good at finessing new money.
Money became her religion, her cloak, her aesthetic.
She embodied it with such ease.
Tight jeans, fur boots, gold chains.
A gold attitude, she called it.
You couldn't tell her nothing or *nada*.
Her style, her energy, her flex was impenetrable.
She was born to be rich. But she was born the wrong
Skin, wrong neighborhood, wrong tax bracket.
Her inheritance was making struggle sexy.
She bought *Vogue* and *Elle* and *Glamour*.
She wore leather jumpsuits and gold shoes and big rings.
She said big things come in small pieces and at 5'5"
People still thought her a giant.
A *grandota* doused in hood galore.
A *matatana* on a mission.
Chanel No. 5 and Elizabeth and her red door.
Macy's and Rocawear and Jimmy Jazz and Rainbows.
Avon and Clinique and African shea butter.
Eyeliner sharp enough to cut.
Red lip bold enough to exist.
Loud like opulence is her last name.
I learned confidence from Mami.
I learned to take up space and mean it.

Name Poem

The thing about my name is it don't roll easy off a dry tongue accustomed to mounting a museum of dead language or dead people. Now watch this name resurrect its ancestors in less than 3 minutes and 10 seconds. Watch it suck the bone marrow of its people buried between the walls of that slaughterhouse you call a mouth. This might make you feel dizzy, but watch this name be feminine and still intersectional. Still respect gender nonconforming names and whichever pronouns they choose to use.

Watch it politicize its stance.
Watch it not vote Trump.
Watch it not make excuses for xenophobia, or racism or sexism.
This name been Making America Great.
Been a conversation starter for diversity and worldly views.
Watch this name root for everybody Black and everybody femme.
Everybody that been ostracized. Left to fend for themselves.

Watch it lean in to your discomfort.
Watch it take up space and not ask for permission.
Watch Melania Luisa do the most. All organic and unfertilized.
Watch it grow its own food. Cure its own cancer. Become its own
    master.

Watch as this name reclaims its time. Waits for you to get it together and clear a path that been there already but, you know, this name stay making an entrance. Stay educating you on conversations of true allyship. This name is a worldly struggle. My grandmothers turning cotton scraps into silk. Is Haiti burning the devil seeds gifted by Monsanto. This name is

Santera. Is Jehovah's witness. Is a witch dressed in a nun's uniform. Doing the work of more than one God, hands here to heal. Is living in purpose so you can die in peace. Is understanding that my mother's country is poor for your country to be rich. Is not accepting white history as fact. Is letting you know this country was built on the backs of the very same people whose names you have trouble pronouncing. But we get it. Melania, too gutter for your allergic gut. Luisa, not here for your consumption. Does not provide a filter for you before you drink it. Lets you chew it up and still climbs its way back out. Is built for and by people with names other than Katie, or George or Donald. This name is not here for your apology—is busy right now living its best life. Too busy to care if you can't stand how "un-American" this name be soundin' in America. So when I say, *No, it's Melania Luisa*, what I mean is, *Watch how gracefully I decolonize my name out your fuckin' mouth*.

Let The Melanated Girl Sleep In
& Stop Inviting Her
To Your Protest

It's Friday.
On Facebook,
there are white women
inviting me to a protest at city hall.

I wish there was a "not interested" button.
Instead, I click "ignore."

I do not wish to be the blockade between them and their lovers.
I am not the bulletproof vest they can lure into a dark room.
I will not fight this battle for them.

I google, how do you say,
"I AM NOT YOUR NEGRO but make it fashion."
I giggle at the nerve of all this performative wokeness.
I wish to say, my tired ass is sleeping in.

At White Parties There's Always A Token-Black-Girl Used As A Couch

Hear me out / she is usually not a couch / to sit on / lean against / her shoulder not exactly the best of cushions / but she's got quite the hips / and honey is sittingggg / claws out / digging into the rug / there is always a colored rug for these occasions / helps catch any white spills / milk / tears / cum / you name it / somewhere a white person will scream reading this poem / all white liquid excretions matter / am i right? / there must always be room for whitesplaining in this poem / how else will the reader have a chance to defend their own mind / they will read this and feel triggered / how does she know? / they will say / i am being attacked! / they will pout / the couch is revolving door / when one black girl gets tired they insert another / a slot machine / full of tokens / here / and here / more of her here / they don't ask for her consent / just sit / be still / good girl / smile / lower that voice / that ass / lower / we need your help / this partayyy would not be so diverse without you / she be so tired / but where can she go / these people claim to be her friends / and what's friendship without safety? / sometimes she remembers her last trip to the token aisle / some / time / like tonight / she'll remember to ask her white friend sarah / will there be other black people there? / sarah being such a sarah will act perplexed and honestly surprised / sarah does not see color / sarah isn't colorblind / sarah says of course and lies / sarah is such an ally / waves her flag so high / sarah thinks she's thoughtful / what she means to say is dense / sarah forgets / sarah doesn't want to remember / most white people have not moved past the burning cross / now the house is on fire / but sarah at least remembered to bring the white wine.

Who Am I?

They watch me to see what kind of woman I'll be. A nasty woman. A bad woman. The kind of woman that don't let herself get taken so easily. A feisty woman. A woman of machetes and undiluted rum. A woman with painful stories and the bravery to claim them.

I'm a sad woman, disillusioned with a country that still barters humans for consumption. On a good day, people walk around me, feigning sentiment for the effortless streetlight of a figurine they made me out to be. They say luck be a lady. I say luck be her liberty.

On my worst day, they prop me up as a symbol of freedom. Can't take me back to where I come from so they settle me onto this mantel. Dress me in the finest of jewels and crown me an emblem of autonomy.

My body is no longer my own but I'm the type of woman who always knew this colonized world ain't never been what it claimed to be.

Soon, they will think me a monument. An example of everything they'll try to forget was human and here I will stand. Feet glued to the ground. My skin, bronzed by the sun. My sky has no ceiling. My torch, still burning for freedom.

MAL HABLA

My mother calls me *mal habla*.
Tells me I have become too angry at the world.
Her Spanish tells me I've changed in all the wrong ways.
Tells me I am angry at them. That I have chosen another side.
Her Spanish tells me what I feel doesn't have the right words.
That I say the wrong things.
A monster inside my mouth.
That I speak in crude tongue.
Tells me I don't know how to be soft,
and I wonder
how much
of myself
is scared
to come
out of
hiding.

Child's Play At A Funeral

Playing is described as a tool to help children develop their imagination, agility, and physical, cognitive and emotional strength. It is through playing that children at an early age are able to interact and engage with the world. I researched to see if the same rule applied for grown-ups. It did. We humans happen to be innately silly. Our blood jiggles and jumps to the tune of fun. Our endorphins butterfly happiness into a heightened state. Our heart becomes warm milk and honey. A sweet exuberance pouncing a light dance of life. Our breath marries nature, suddenly able to exceed a light resting point, an infinite energy.

I was 7 the last time I saw my father. I remember him as the most playful man I have ever known. A gentle giant, someone who saw the world and all its woes and still believed in good. His funeral, a family reunion. Us kids are all playing in confusion and excitement. Running around the grass, playing tag inside the church. My polka-dot dress stained a leafy green. The sun, still glorious and shiny as ever. The adults fanning themselves out of heat exhaustion. Sweating more than they were crying. Between bouts of crying and then forgetting why I was crying. We laid him to rest.

I was 10 the first time I realized I would never see him again. It was June and everyone was excited for the end of sixth grade. I had just explained to my best friend, Shanice, that people die and my father was dead. That he won't be attending my elementary school graduation. That he can no longer come out and play with me anymore. That he was a good guy who loved feeding the squirrels peanuts, his favorite vegetable iceberg lettuce. That the only song I had ever heard him sing was from a cassette tape of salsa songs from the '90s in his smelly, gas-guzzling station wagon. My answers to her questions made me feel like such a grown-up. Like a cool girl who was ready for middle school. Who no longer needed recess to run around and play. Until it dawned on me, I was worried about him. Does my father, wherever he is, ever get to play? Where does all the fun go when you die? And when I die, will we get to play together again?

After his funeral, I spent the rest of that summer running barefoot in the rain, trying to feel connected to the island he loved so much. An island of a home. God, what a heavenly home. I rejoice when I think of how we mourned his death. I think we did it the way any child of his would. By playing. Our fondest memories of him were of parks and jungle gyms. He always watched in amazement. In another life, if I ever get the chance to run around the park with him again, I hope each time he'll join me.

I know the boy in him was always playing too.

On Becoming

The divinity of the universe
never failed her and yet,
she grew skeptical.
We don't know when God
became a storm she feared
but here she was,
a disheveled palm tree,

uprooted.

Girl Power

P.S. 134 on the Lower East Side, NYC

If you could go back, would you
Crawl slow into that velvet blue couch
And sing, sing until bedtime—*girl power!*

You feel the coordination & calcium—and dance
Chocolate milk one hand, gel brush in other.
You sing and twirl and sing and pose
The way Ashanti and your mirror taught you.
Between the Cheetah Girls & you is a closeness.
Out of necessity sprung visibility, magenta & fur
Among little girls across America.

We believed the truth because we needed it
We bought the soundtrack, so hungry for home
And home is not always familiar or warm.
Sometimes it is a curious hip awaiting a hand
A shimmy, shimmy cocoa pop from four mouths
With hyperpigmented lips who speak like you
Dance like you, love like you, and want to live
This leopard-print promised land just like you.

If you could go back, the safety of innocence
Awaiting your tender crown—greasing regal
Scalp full of Vaseline and a promising song

That you exist safely in a future—belly round
Full of stardom, direction and dreams.

You girl, are exactly where you need to be, warmed up.
You girl, are always on time and always on beat,
And always got style and finesse down to a T.
You girl, got power—girl power.

On Colorism

I was 12 the first time I realized my friends and I see the world differently. Somewhere between looking in the mirror and looking at people around me, I learned to see in color. I learned words can be armor and skin can break friendships. My best friend and I were not talking. It all began with a comment she made about a Black girl and her attitude. She claims it must've been because she's jealous of her hair and her pretty. I told her that may have been the case like it could be the case that she doesn't like you. She asked *why you always defending Black girls for?* So I said *why you always shitting on Black girls for?* Why is it always us versus them? Always Black vs mixed vs white. It's always *she just mad 'cause I got good hair* and *all the boys want me. Don't you see me? I look like all the pretty girls on TV. I look like the trophy wives.* Look like something worth cherishing. Like someone worth loving. *That's why all the boys have been raised to respect and love me.* Not that dark brown skin. Only pale skin. Only slight curly hair. Only mixed blood. Something always got to get put down so that she can build herself up. I ask *why should I have to choose between me and you when we are one?* I ask *where did you learn to pick at Black girls for being Black?* I ask *why does that make you feel good?* I tell her, culture for us is something we can't take off. You can choose which part of your culture you wish to celebrate. You can choose between Puerto Rican or Dominican or American. But my skin isn't disposable. My skin is a shade I'm forced to side with, to mend, to hold tightly, the way it holds me like a hug. My skin is shea butter melting with the warmth of pressed hands on sun-kissed thighs. Looking up, I am worthy and loved despite the ache. I release this burden. How easy it is for her to pass as whatever. To be Spanish and seen. I tell her, *I'm sorry if my Black is showing.* If I won't let her chew the parts of me I can't hide. If my skin makes her feel uncomfortable. If I become partial to this brown. If my Blackness is a deal breaker. If it makes me see the world differently. If I don't allow her to use colorism as a shield for self-esteem. If I choose to love this melanin as a gift, not a curse. If my skin doesn't burn in the sun. If my skin glows. If my skin shines. If it comes home.

My America / Mi Tierra

My America, a *sancocho* of broken English, train rides
and calling cards. The *frío fríos* on Delancey Street.
The two-dollar Two Boots pizza and soda school specials.
The summer walks along the FDR Drive.
There was no hood safer than mine. No hood happy as mine.
The *abuelitas* gossiping out front and keeping us safe.
They stare and smile and pray and pout.
This tierra, not really feeling much like *tierra*.
Too much concrete to feel but we tried our best.
The *salsa* across the street at the retirement home.
The parks are full of barbecue and *moro de gandules*.
My mother's longing for home, a nostalgia that kept her alive.
Our summers *en el campo*, a utopian dream.
When they come looking for us, all they will
find is scraps and memories we left to redeem.

> *Mi tierra* is the right side of a tiny island in the middle
> of the Caribbean Sea. Everyone is clapping when the
> plane lands, harmonious prayers and humble palm raising.
> *Mi tierra* taste like sugarcane and passion fruit,
> taste like the perfect summer day and the perfect
> summer night outside with candles lit and
> no electricity soon in sight. We sit and tell stories
> that make us glint our teeth in belly quakes.
> *Mi tierra* is being barefoot in a hammock
> eating *tostones* and sipping soursop.
> *Mi Tierra* is mine.
> *Mi Tierra* is mine.
> *Mi Tierra* is mine.

Ode To The New York Public Library

You saved me. I hope you know that. I hope you remember
my deep laugh lines and undiluted joy. Remember that
time a mentor gave me a pin that said *Reading is
FUNdamental* and we were soooooo hype. And I ran
home all the way from school the next day just to show
you. I spent that day reading a romantic comedy in your
love chair.

You always knew humor and love were my safe space. You,
my safe space. You and those sweet librarians. Always
found ways to reduce my late fines or gift me a fresh new
library card. I, too embarrassed to say I kept my favorite
books because I could never afford the Scholastic fair to
own them.

Remember those lovely Saturday mornings? When I got
grown enough to walk to your doorstep by myself. I
would skip and prance after a belly full of pancakes and
orange juice.

Remember that backpack so heavy your spines near broke
my back? I'm not saying you the reason I have scoliosis; I'm
saying if chronic back pain is the price to pay for having
you, wordsmith god, literary queen, alphabetized deity.

I'd slouch and bend and snap all over again
I'd scour the earth searching for you
How you bind me free,

your aisles, your pages,
you rudimentary savior.

You bring me home.
Each time I doubted
I was going to make it,
you read me anew.

L.E.S / D.R.

Island city girl. A diaspora baby.
Tangled between here and there.
Her lineage, an urban tale she
still searches for the meaning of.

A New York Summer

I wasn't born in the summer but I always come alive around this time. Those who live through a New York Summer learn to encapsulate four seasons' worth of sun and fun into one.

There is no time to waste for winter blues are always one sappy, melodic beat away. Reminding us of the woes and ash from which we have risen. So we learn to waste no time.

Learn to *dance with somebody, feel the heat with somebody.* Even if they ask, *What's my name?* And you have absolutely no idea, you turn to the next song and sing, *If you want me to stay, I'll never leave.* And you *lean back* into that truth, that you are enamored with a city and its addictive magnetic pulse. They might call you *crazy in love* to which you'll always have the rhythm and the range to reply, *Yes, I'm from New York, New York.*

Because leaving a New York Summer for anything else is foolish. Leave her in the winter. Leave her when she has nothing good for your heart and your soul. Leave her after you've loved her past her peak. Leave her when she tells you to leave because she knows she can be no good. Leave her when the sun too decides to go. Leave a note, a long kiss goodbye. But promise her that you won't leave forever.

Ode To Amara La Negra

To the Black girls that be Black girls until they open they mouth and speak anything but English. Ode to the way we learned to smirk at the term *immigrant* and *foreign*. Ode to the way we learned to reject the notion that we are "alien" or "illegal" on God-given land. Ode to the telling of stories that always go unwritten. To the families whose sacrifices always go unnoticed. Ode to telling people to fuck off in two colonized tongues. To the Afro-Latinas who don't identify as Afro-Latina because even that sounds Eurocentric. Ode to reminding people that the *Afro* comes before *Latina*. Ode to resisting the task of making your Blackness more digestible. To you discovering the history of colonization, whitewashing and erasure in the Caribbean and across the diaspora. Ode to you learning that Univision and most media are a White-Ass-Lie. To the reclaiming of culture. To the way you learned to take up all this space. To the way you learned to speak for yourself. The way you learned to cook up and serve your own spicy dish. To the *café con leche*. To the *dulce de chinola* and the *plátano maduro*. The warm scent of *manteca*. Ode to you teaching yourself to come out of hiding. To embrace the reflex in your hips on a conga beat. Ode to the Yoruba you never learned that haunts the Spanish in your blood. To the blood that longs for home. Ode to the war that longs for peace. Ode to the question that will always need answering. When they ask, What's it like: to carry the blood of the colonizer and the colonized? To know that there is a war of power inside you that might never heal? To still love yourself despite the trauma? To fight to be seen despite the erasure? To hold your ancestors' dreams of freedom and jump into the unknown?

Homecoming

After Victoria Santa Cruz's
"Me Gritaron Negra!"

Here.
My name is already on the list.
They do not ask for papers.
My Royalty is
enough.

Here, I do not need to prove my humanity.
They do not ask me to kneel at their feet.
They will not scrape my tongue for proof of the rain.
They do not need me to dance in the puddles.

Here, I am Black before I am anything.
I am loved like my life matters.
I am more than the tired I carry.

Here, I know beauty does not come
at the expense of denying my ancestors.
It is because of them.

Proclamó que aunque sea Dominicana, nací Negra.
Proclamó que la vida es única pero el linaje es infinito.
Y esa es la clave secreta.
Y las puertas se abren libremente.
El sancocho ya está hecho,
los mangos caen del cielo,
y Dios celebra mi reencarnación.
y Dios celebra quien soy Negra.

PART TWO

A HISTORY
OF
PLANTAINS

Introduction

The story of the Dominican Republic and Haiti is an origin story of the Americas as colonial as they come. Before Hispaniola, this land was called Quisqueya, a Caribbean island inhabited by Indigenous natives called Taínos. The division into two countries began in the 1600s when France forced itself into the western part of the island of Hispaniola where Spain, through massacres and enslavement, had gained power and rule.* Both France and Spain used the human trafficking and enslavement of Africans for free labor to milk the island for all its bountiful worth. Haiti and the Dominican Republic share a border where Afro-descendants face language barriers as well as varying qualities of life depending on the resources and economic stability the countries have to offer. The Dominican Republic, being a greener and lusher form of colonial paradise and due to having whitewashed its depiction of its citizens and culture, has attracted much more attention from the United States and European countries, making it a prime vacation spot.

Many of its descendants have been displaced by a crooked history. One that told us we were once slaves instead of enslaved. One that told us we were products of strife instead of greed. One that told us we should hate our roots instead of growing ten thousand more. There is a stillness that surrounds God's children when they refuse the burden of the wrongdoer. To be born Black is to be born with an irrefutable spirit, a passion for life and profound lungs that strive to take in the deep green breath of our

---

*"An Island Divided: What the World Must Learn of Tragedy on Hispaniola." Duke Nicholas School of the Environment. April 9, 2014. https://sites.nicholas.duke.edu /loribennear/2014/04/09/612/

creator. Still, in the midst of so many storms, when we listen to the quiet of Mother Earth, there is a message reminding us that we belong and that we have everything we need within us to become.

In *Plantains and Our Becoming*, I have found my roots. I have gone back to the river. I have bowed to the sun. I have spoken to my elders and I have written down my truth. Sometimes, in moments where I lose my breath, I begin to remember how we, *those born the color of earth*, make it back home. Home is where our truth is found. This truth, one scattered across continents and oceans, high up in the mountains, deep in the whispers of the flowy rivers, and forever between the crevices of this labored soil. This truth is that of love and reinvention. This truth emanates from dust and diamonds pulsing with pressure and demands we greet our ancestors with more than a conditioned reality. The truth is that *we know Earth like we know survival*.

There is no blueprint for our existence. We choose. We rise like a root from the other side conjuring words that were never meant for our tongues to articulate. We dig up blood memories that both shatter and thicken our skin & spirit. We learn. We dance. We fall in love with ourselves and our survival again, and again, and again. And we refuse to go back to the unknowing. For to be without culture is to be without spirit.

Synonyms For Stolen People

Once African.   Once rooted.
Now confused.   Now floating.

                 Tragic Spirit.
                     Where you from?
Negra Bella   How you still Black?
       Negro Lindo
                         What got 'chu so uptight?

Hijxs de Dios
                 What 'chu so mad 'bout?

Where yo' people from?   How free is you?   How Black is you?

                 Voodoo Black?
                 Plantain Black?
                 Sugarcane Black?

What island yo' ancestors drown in?
How you surrounded by water and scared to float?
Which side will your privilege choose?
How you reckon you'll translate this unknowing?
What of the border between your river?
What of the tired within your bones?

You must remember that, although stolen, you have always been saved.

The Gospel Of Plantains

Plantains like most sacred things do not know borders.
They know Earth like they know survival.
They know how to split themselves in 10,
how to ransack, pillage, morph into something a white devil can't kill.

In the beginning, there was light, and love, and land
and no one had to die to come home.
But America loves to make a bloody crucifix out of me.
Tells me my American penance is my Black body riddled with bullets.
Tells me this is the price I must pay for my own freedom.

Still, I shake off the devil by twerking when I feel tense.
On Sundays, I nap as if it were blasphemy to refuse this sway of answers.
How, you ask? By making life a ritual, my body a reclamation,
my spirit an infinite TikTok dance.
Like *plátanos*, I too know how to let the wind shake me loose.

Because my body is the Black parade.
Because I come from women with hips that spread.
Not like butter. Like *batatas*. We rooted and stubborn.
Who love themselves like bathing in an ocean of sea and white cloths.
What is church if not the sweet song of flowering water as you eat
root vegetables the same celestial way your ancestors did?
We God things conjure memory through taste, sweat, rhythm and rest.
Watch as we nap and dance our way back into our future.

Questions For Hispaniola

Before you were a border,   Before you were meek,
   you were one island,   you were called savage,
     you were freeland.   you were called slave empire.
What changed? (2x)

Who are your assassins? Who is your savior?
What should we do with your children?
Teach me your history. Show me something real.
We are watching you, lovely. We have been waiting for your movement.
Wishing that you raise your machete. Arm us with answers.
Pick a stance and bring us to freedom. We are waiting on your sweet
song of revolution. Teach me your liberty.
Tell us if we must die for this right.
What a divine sacrifice that would be.

You could've been a haven for Africa's children, *why the betrayal?*
Why are you silent? What drives you? Your children's bodies in the streets,
do you not see?

Who is lodged in between your throat? Have you forgotten how to scream?
Why won't you tell the world the truth? Have they sewn your mouth shut?
Have they taxed you too deep? Do they owe us a new island? Tell me,
please: Where can we go to escape this tired?

Por favor, vuelve Mamá Tingó
Retounen, Toussaint Louverture
Vuelve, Ana María

Vuelve, Pablo Alí
Retounen, Jean-Jacques Dessalines
Return.

Teach us to be freedom fighters, if only while we sleep.
Teach me. Teach me to be an assault rifle.
To conjure your rage with palo muerto.
Teach me to pray as much as I curse.
Teach me to choose violence.
Teach me to be a root. To stand firm in something.
Anything. There is no wrong way to want to make it out alive.

Isla Cuentos / Hood History 101 / It's All About The Money, Honey

1492 Christopher Columbus, his ashy self, sailed the ocean blue. Columbus helped Spain plot and scheme and steal and kill. Santo Domingo became its first victim. And what's a colonizer gonna do? Keep finding land and resources to steal. Over two hundred years of bullshit. France and Spain throw hands over the island and France steals Haiti while Spain steals the Dominican Republic. Both savage empires beat, dehumanize and force enslaved Africans to work for free and exploit the island's resources. And that's why I'm always like, Reparations when? Because open thy purse like y'all pried open our land. African descendants led the revolution against France in Haiti and in 1804, Saint Domingue got free. Haiti was indubitably the world's first nation birthed by enslaved Africans and that's on period. No cap. No need for discussion. Their uprising caused a ripple effect across the Americas. The Dominican Republic got free from Spain in 1821. I know that's right, but a chaotic entanglement with Haiti began. DR was all like, Don't mess with my money, honey. And Haiti still had France's anti-Black debt looming over their economy. And the bills needed to get paid. So things got messy. And this is what nationalists have used to pit the two countries against each other. The root is layers of colonialism, enslavement, poverty and a persistent "crabs in a barrel" mentality. Everybody wanna be on the winning team. Everybody wanna get free. Everybody here waiting on they 40 acres and they mule.

Loca, esa gente ni se bañaban. Y vino Colombo con su grajo y to' a joder pa'ca. Y como bueno sucios que son eso Españoles mataron pila de indígenas para adueñarse de la isla. La vaina se puso fea con eto grajoso peleando por la isla. Una vaina fuerte. Un movie fatal. Yo te digo a ti que por eso no se puede confiar. Encima de que matan casi to' lo Indígenas con su grajo y mala vibra y sus plagas. Siguen los Españoles y los Frances azarándole la vida a uno. Así de fácil vienen eso desgraciado a traer Africanos esclavizados a trabajar pa'que ello ten chillin'. Esa gente tiene una vagancia del diablo. Desde los 1492. Pero eso fue hasta un día. To' eso tiguere de Haiti se fajaron. Quemaron tierra, agarraron machete y lucharon, pana. Hasta el final. Y cuando por fin no dieron independencia, como quiera no dieron en la madre. En Haiti le sacaron to' el jugo lo France cobrándole un dineral por ser libre al fin. Entonces la republica se zapatio de España, pero vino a caer en un huidero con Haiti. Loco yo te digo a ti, adonde hay tierra, hay problema. Imagínate, Haiti con esa deuda grandísima a Francia, que podia ello hacer por uno? RD no tuvo de otra que escapársele. Porque si no se jode todo. Al fin, por eso es que todavía tamo tenso de los dos lados. Eto'ni un dembow chulo puede suavizar. Señore oren y busquen de Dios por que no se sabe adónde vallemos a parar. To' el mundo quiere ganar. To' el mundo quiere libertad. To' el mundo aquí ta esperando su 40 tarea y su mula.

The Country Is Black But Our President Is White

They pave a new street before the president comes into town.
And we laugh, the pavement still won't be ready in time.
For us. It will never by ready in time. Not for her, them, or he, not
    like this.
It's been so long since last time, they forgot how long pavement takes
    to dry.
It's obvious we all get lost in the thick of black sticky tar.
Neighborhoods in ~~you~~ who want to be heard but no one to listen.
Motorcycles and *pasolas* complained for years. Tired from horsing
People on broken infrastructure. I ~~don't~~ think it's healthy to be this
Forgotten or forsaken. The potholes got us robbed before we could
    speed.

The government got us robbed before we could even see. I ~~find~~ it
Problematic to blame us for having no other choice.
~~You don't find that suspicious?~~ They blame the hole.
The street with only one way in and one way out. The dead end.
The earth it came from. The poverty that sprung. Blame the lie. Blame.
Blame us for needing our money in our neighborhoods pouring concrete.
When it rains, the holes become an ocean's cave for worms to swim free.
When it's hot, the holes watch women in the backseat drive off with
Men who offer cold fruity liquor and *pesos* in exchange for sweet &
    good times.
When it's cold, the holes watch people burn tires and block the road.
Remind the mayor we have nothing to lose if we can't even make
    it home.

To be honest, I am not ~~that~~ observant. I just know basic math.
When a thing is a thing that just don't add up.
1 country does not need to be under siege to be desperately in need
    4 reform.
My life is not an equal exchange & that's why we here. 7 feet deep in
The poetics of potholes and the lies of dirt that won't stick.

Them potholes keep secrets and duck bullets & beasts.
It's no mystery who the greedy monsters are. Is it?
Thieves who hide between sentences and teeth.
All of what these streets have seen, ~~suspicious~~ politicking ghosts
Tap-dancing in suits to the tune of famished beats.
This tired got us shackled, feet frozen in our own asphalt.
What would they do if they had no one beneath them to step on?
Visit our *barrio* tiptoeing over wet cement. Wear hard hats and ride
Around bulletproof *Jeepetas* asking us to smile for patience.
Good things take time and bad people take even more.
Measure the potholes and see how much deeper they be.
3 pandemic years later & still we wait. Sudden acts of "kindness"
Let you know when vampires are ready to show their fangs.
I'm not even sure I know enough about politics to write this poem.
But I am a Black thing covered in dirt standing her ground.
So I speak even if no one will listen. And no one will listen.
~~You don't find that suspicious?~~

The Haitian & Dominican Flag Exchange Words

They do not ask,
just hunt.
I become the bullet and the gun.
Somehow you still run from me.
Where is my paradise?
Won't you meet me at the river?
Grab a rosary,
sing to me,
it is the only time we are one.
Feed me your national hymn,
make me believe you. I
embarrass you
but I cannot pretend to be
something I am not.
You blame me,
not the wretched white man.
You claim *tres razas*
but our tree is Black.
6,000-year-old wisdom.
There is room for both of us.
Meet me under our Black.

If I am weary,
blame a white God.
Taught to haunt myself to sleep.
They latched this stallion to my back.
I suffocate under his colossal weight.
You have to believe me,
I did not create this beast of hate,
an inheritance.
How can I say no to them? They
give me entry to the world.
Learn to see past color, made us invisible.
A wall between our hearts.
A coward stealing our jewels.
And profit off my head spins,
our island lost.
I'm sorry—gave up,
the want to come home.
It's been so long,
I've forgotten.
But how?
Are we safe here?

Land Of Mountains, Tourism
& Lambónismo

The Dominican Republic & Haiti receive
more than 6 million tourists per year;
Christopher Columbus is said to have been the first.
The first to reach someone else's paradise and call it yours.
The one to pillage and persecute and then become a national hero.
His statue stands mighty and tall in Santo Domingo.
To be the first slave port of the Americas and to be romantically
     entangled
With your colonizer is to master the art of *lambónismo*.

Gold pendants atop a garden of armor
and this country is said to be alive and well.
A paradise for those who tour along the beach
but won't dare enter its jungles without at least
six police cars trailing or paying off the government.
Or trading gold for asylum.
They say that when this land goes under water
they will send boats or planes.
Small enough for one percenters whose children study in Europe.
Won't dare get a degree from a country under siege. Or ruin.
Death plaguing the countryside. Swollen babies fat
with the salt of invasive poachers. I mean tourists.
I mean curious eyes. I mean stargazing for gold mines.
I mean contaminating the river water, polluting the air.
I mean, it's no wonder our world is always ending.

We, children of *plátanos*, always gotta learn to play in everyone else's backyard and somehow feel at home. They always find a way to pilfer and spoil what was natural for good reason. What if the land and the fruit were forbidden from us so that we may die? And if you choose to not die, how will they label you then?

Internalized & Anti____

just say it. say when you see a haitian person
island-talk, they remind you of africa. say you don't
want to be reminded of why you're here. say you were
told if they survived it was the devil's spite. say it scares
you that your god was wrong. say voodoo is just the
bible rephrased. say you fear they are more of god's
children than you. say your religion is hidebound.

say your version of god is bigotry. say your prayer
for abundance is someone else's genocide. say your
prayer for safety is someone else's displacement. say
your policing of humans is someone else's pipeline/
terror/haunting. say your country is sitting on top of
bones. say the ghosts are more than just in your head.

say your nationalism is biased. say your church has
the hunted blood of ancestors on their hands. say
your denial is death. say your language is intrusive.
say your words know no bounds. say you fear the
translation. say kreyol is patois is igbo is swahili is yo-
ruba is zulu is portuguese is english is spanish is the
rolling of a hard *r* and an invisible *l* in a language
only black people learned to speak and scream.

say you learned more about your killer than your
hero. say your language is more than just a barrier or
a border. say your language is a cage.

say your language is your master,
                      is your monster,
                      is your mother,

frail and tired.
crying into her eucalyptus tea.
desperately rocking herself to sleep at night.
begging you to stop breaking her tender heart and finally
                                          come on home.

If I Could Buy All My Homies
An Island / Where They At?

Bring 'em out bring 'em out. Bring me your refugees, your undocumented, your displaced, your misplaced, your headache, your unclaimed, and uncalled, and unfinished soldiers. Bring 'em out. Tell them I saved them an island. Tell them to hurry quick. Bring me your invisible, your embarrassment, your discarded, your disabled, your unprotected and unloved. The ones you make legislation against. The ones you pipeline into a carceral state. Your battered, your bruised, your prisoners of colonial inheritance. Your unraveled, your unlearning, your divested and decolonial. Your hungry and hunkered and having to beg for home. Your genius and gorgeous and golden and gangsta and ghetto. Bring me your truth, your culture, your sauce. If you don't want to love them. Tell them I will. I will love them because they have always been mine to adore and hold. This stream of endearment is a kingdom we have always known. The map was lost but we fear not. We will find our way back to each other.   Bring them.   Bring 'em out.   We have saved them an island. They need to see. A global majority that looks just like them.

In Harlem
    In the Bronx
        In Houston
            In Louisiana
                In Miami
                    In Hialeah
                        In Oakcliff
                            In Compton
                                In Atlanta
                                    In Jersey City

In South Carolina
In Austin
In Rio de Janeiro
In the DMV
In Colombia
In the Southside
In Azua
In Sosúa
In Bonao

In Haiti, we everywhere and that is the problem. But it ain't their business yet they made it so. It's why they stay mad. It's the tickle in their salty throat. How they spit and slur. What of the dead who don't stay dead? Who conjure, clunk, bow and rise. What of the sea in amniotic fluid? There's an umbilical cord that used to be a chain, now a root. They wish to bleach the coral to bone, peel the plantains of all pigment, boil into chlorophyll and quench their thirst. They clean the knives of this history but the forest remembers. The plantations remember. The spirits remember. The ocean remembers. Here is a bright ecosystem of people who will always find a way to endure. What of that thin veiled speck of brown light got you in an uproar? Your conquest is a reflection of your fears, my dear. Get out of your own way and collect your memories. Even the ones you wish to vomit. Even the ones who keep you brick-eyed and spasming in the hammock that is your throat. Unclench your fist and roll out the beauty in your fragile palm. In your genes are a paper trail. You will find a map back to yourself.

We may all have the same God but we don't have the same mother.

I Trace Back My Black
So Ancestry.com
Don't Take My Money

I say Africa because I just don't know. I don't know the exact root of this Black. This Black is just my truth. What has become of me. What I have always been. What I embody. Generalized and unspecified but the feeling is universally known. Somewhere there is a woman cosplaying as me, calling herself transracial, and it stings just the way neocolonialism is supposed to sting. It's supposed to kill like a quiet war. Like bombings that don't make the news. Like refugees who are too Black to be victims. It's supposed to kill just like they like it to. When they wear the trendiness of our skin and style. When they sing our songs and dance our beats. When they wear our ancestors as their own. It stings because far too long we have been their money maker, their circus, their mule. My unknowing, their triumph. My search, their child's play. My insecurity, their comedy. The first tear is most venomous. I cry about it sometimes. *I just don't know. I long to know. I long to know.* But I'll never know because anything that could prove my family's passage was burned during *la revolución*. All I have are stories from my elders and vibes. All I have is *cuentos de hada* and what the spirits tell me. There are no documents that can prove my root so I make it up. My friend tells me, *Listen, babe, whatever we were before the boat ride must've been magnificent.* So here is my magnificent family tree:

My great-great-grandmother ———— My great-great-grandfather
the brilliant, the rice farmer,
the dancer, the *curandera* the sweet melody hummer

My great-grandmother ———— My great-grandfather
the cacao farmer, the politician,
the matriarch, the hustler,
the diamond in the rough the joyous statuesque & handsome

My grandmother ———— My grandfather,
the seamstress, the God lover, the electrical engineer,
the first on U.S. soil, the life of the party,
the eye of beauty the humble giant

My father,
the teacher, the mechanic,
the best hugger

My grandmother, ———— My grandfather
the cook, the sex worker, the miner, the guitarist
the healer, and singer, the sweet
the spitting image and suave romantic
of Mother Earth

My mother,
the fighter, the beautician,
the visionary,
my first home

Eco-Hood

i learned environmentalism from my hood.
i learned sustainability from my hood.
i learned to be frugal and fly from my hood.
i learned to reuse tupperware, repurpose t-shirts,
tie plastic bags to my head.
this be a shower cap, an umbrella, luggage,
a container for more bags.
this be a conversation starter, an educational tool,
a reminder to do what you can with what you got.

i learned environmentalism from my hood.
i learned to make aluminum jars pretty vases and pencil holders.
i learned to not hoard, to be creative, to be brilliant.
i learned scraps of wood make tables from my cousin manolo.
i learned t-shirts can be dishrags from my mother-in-law.
i learned to throw seeds back into soil from my abuelita.

i learned they blame the hood and not the heist by conglomerates.
i learned that the most vulnerable are the most targeted.
i learned real taste is not taxable, only renewable.
you can't buy this kind of intrinsic desire to make
one man's trash another man's dream.
at the edge of a landfill is a hood repurposing waste.
my favorite environmentalists don't call themselves
environmentalists, they just honor the earth and the land.

Hecha Completa

There are resorts on the island where the women vacation in hospital beds. Closets of *fajas*, sutures, IV fluids, disinfecting gauze, soup containers, and massage oil. Enter and all becomes one big fat blur. Like factories, Barbies enter waxy blobs of insecurities and exit *hecha completa*. A flesh piñata of new skin, new body, new attitude. Suddenly they hear *beautiful* and believe it. They hear *bad bitch* and think, *Me, it's possible. To be as flawless as I wanna be. To own my body and a part of this Earth. To demand equity and power.* They can finally look in the mirror and see value, see a whole woman unbutchered by the stench of rumoring flies and flaws. What does it mean to be cut open in order to be made complete?

•

When I say *beautiful*, what I mean is the thread of my body is unraveling itself into a war factory of roses. May they stain and scare all those who dare touch. My body hears *perfect* and morphs into a pink submachine gun. My waist hears *invisible* and snatches itself into a belt of spikes. My lips hear *lovable* and grind the tears of ex-lovers into dust. My body smiles with sharpened teeth unflinching and on. What does it mean to weaponize your body in order to bear the weight of this existence?

•

In cases of prewar, an increase in war probability tends to decrease stock prices but the ultimate outbreak of war increases them. There are empty factories of machinery waiting for their value to be appreciated. Our bodies are waiting to be appreciated. How they hold all our insides and then some. How they forgive the butcher and reprieve the soul. Some folks need war to feel peace and sometimes swallowing all that has tried to kill us is enough. What does it mean to need trauma to feel alive?

•

It's brave, you know. To know the pain and choose it every single time. As long as the rent gets paid and the babies get fed, and luxury is within reach. As long as someone sees this body and thinks it worth loving, worth fighting a war, worth exchanging money for. What does it mean to be a working body in a society that demands perfection?

•

When I was sixteen, I wished for a nose job and lipo. I never told my mother who could barely afford to gift me life that I wanted to be just like her. *Hecha completa*. With a body that was either made by God or godly made. Grant me access to pretty things from which to thrive. If we could eat beauty, how delicious it would be. To devour all the lovely and finally feel complete. What does it mean to the human condition to fix what is never enough?

•

When our bodies talk, how violent it be.

La Matatana Cibaeña

abuelita checks on me every rise   _   same way
she walks her garden to resurrect dead leaves
whisper,   compliment
holy herbs.   her one true love has always been
          earth.
men   were her chew toys.
ornaments   _   dance partners
she slung on hip   or   arm
never could quite   figure   out
what she didn't like about them.
something about them.
their bite,   their obsessive love,
their need for control of the feminine.
and yet she found them to be so basic so boring
they   do the bare minimum & cities get named
in honor. God rises, in image.
She wonders   when
              woman became
bad   _   religion?

Where God Lives

in the spirit of
Dominican women
as they light up a small room
dancing *bachata* without
ever lifting a foot off the ground.

Why We Pray

moon after moon, i sit to speak with you, reassuring
    myself
that prayer is not only a poor crazy person's therapy.
my knees fall, gentle as to not break the glass that is
    my faith.
to find the strength to pray on the things i cannot change.
it begins and ends with black ink.
the dye of sorrows left unanswered or unopened.
night leaves drag my words into dusk.
hope a tree forms in the morning.
a branch for each of my people. my loves.
my heart. the ones who squeeze daylight out of me
the ones who pour into me when i am all dried out.
when i wish to be more palm tree than cacti
who drag the sunshine back into my teeth.

today, god i am not holy, just real and worried.
i don't want to die in a country that won't welcome
my mother home
won't kiss her calloused hands seeking asylum
won't greet the desperation in her eyes
will strip her of humanity for being poor and brown.

a mother mourns her child being lynched today.
today, her babies are confiscated from her womb
for being alien instead of patriot.

today, a father learns he is masochistically married
to a country that only wants his body
if he doesn't have a soul or a family
or the joy of seeing seeds you planted
bloom in uncharted land
land you blessed with your tired and martyred hands.

instead, rosaries snatched off their necks get sent to cross
a border with nothing but the melanin on their backs
and a bill of rights they need translated.

they will deport them and keep their babies.
send them back to a country she refused
to raise children in
cursed land
bloody government
unstable infrastructure
refused to let her kids go missing.

who will translate their mourning?
who will sing her babies their last lullaby?
who will protect her child from the white monsters in suits.
what godforsaken curse are we still drowning ourselves
       trying to break?

must swallow this knot in our throats and call it holy water.
call it a baptism. call it proof of you.

Untitled

Abuelita says,
Gracias a Dios, aquí nunca
pasa nada tan terrible.

And I know it's just
a matter of geography and luck.

What she means to say is,
we are not environmental
refugees just yet. . . .

Mashing Plátanos

coddle them with praying hands
remember they were born   hanging
not like fruit but like bodies dragged
into boats & shipped as cargo
propped crates, bonded limbs,
groups of 5 or 10 standing upright
fresh for sale.

before you begin to cut,
it is tradition to oil   hands
do not disturb the flesh.
cut and detach
yourself from the lineage
of all of this.

be gentle &   witness
the greed & glory in nature,
find solace in carrying
on with life,
no answers but one.

as they lay in your boiling pot naked,
salt the water to taste. somewhere
between folklore & dark matter &   delicacy
grab your holiest mixing pot,
the one your abuelita makes mangú in.

to mash plantains is to remember
you hold history in the palms of your hands.

sweat if you must, watch hot vapor   rise.
spin your breath & muscle,
mash earth into therapy,
still & present.

Dem Dog Dayz Are Ova

i want to be shocked every single time. i want to cry about it every single time. i want to fight about it every single time. as long as i do not become numb to this hell. to this lie. to this hate. this depletion. this whip or this gun. glocked at my neck. got me questioning my own heaven and my own love. in the thick of my arched spine, i remember that at the very least i still have a spine and that bitch refuses to break. i want to be shocked. i want to be appalled. baffled. encroached. consumed. anything but complicit or numb. anything but docile or defective. i want to be present in my demise and let it be known i peeped. i prepped. i refused. i never want to be a ghost to my suffering. i want to feel it all. i want to be shocked every single time they tell me this what i'm worth. this none. this speck. me. child of god. green goblin. ethereal thing. she who moves with hips of an ocean and hair thick as seaweed. she who speak and let universe listen. she with an hourglass body and buttered skin. she whose spirit time travels through quicksand. she be an island. divinely created in her glory. perfected in this light. she, her, i, they, we. we refuse. we sharpened and unflinching. i have all and all of me been waiting. i am not immune or exempt. i bide my time. i would do it over again. as long as i do not let the world think for one second i am swallowing in submission. i will never submit. bow. side. this kind of verdict will always be unjust. and i will always let it be known. i want to scream about it every single time. every time they tell me i am cursed. every time they spit on me. spit on my roots. spit on my seed. every time they tell me my life does not matter. i want to yell at the top of my lungs in spite. i want to open my arms and dive into its watery hell. i want to bathe in its waters and let it keep me. for as long as it wants so it can see i will not drown. not how they want me to. not today like they insist. not now. not for them. not for their gaze or prize. not for their joy. not for their meal or their playtime. i will not drown. nor will i die. not on their watch. not for their pleasure. i was born floating. i was born knowing this whole damn time. i am no victim and nobody's fuckin' martyr and nobody's doormat or dog. i am no dog. and them dog dayz been over. shout out to that white woman. she know what she be singin' and she know she betta say that shit with her whole goddamn chest. i be sayin' this here with my whole goddamn chest. on some eat pray love tip. i believe in it and i never flinch. or duck. or lie. this real, and this truth here mine. i am not immune nor exempt but i sure damn am refusing. i will it and i refuse it until the day that i die. and believe me when i say, i rather goddamn die than swallow this venom. this spite keeps me. this lust for bitter truth. this truth here mine. i deserve to be mine. i am always mine. on my terms. on my life. on my joy. my freedom. my free. i be so hungry for my kind of free. a meal eaten raw. i chew and spit and no way swallow their shit. i was not put on this earth to eat shit. there is no convincing this body of anything other than exactly what it is here to do. to exist despite. not because or as a product of. but purely because it was meant to be. and i don't know by who or by what. sometimes i'm not even sure if we will continue to exist and carry on. this future, mine. what i do know is that we exist in the now and we exist in my future. and we exist to love. and we exist to laugh. and we exist to care for each other for a second, or a minute, or forever. and right now all i want is to focus on the now. in the now i am whole and refusing. and i exist. not by coincidence or by chance. but by miracle. somebody had to dream me up. whole and loving. whole and with child. all dreamt up. up and whole and refusing to let them kill my seed. in the now. i exist. and the green of us exist too. and we refuse and it may very well cost us our life. but this, who are we without it? without the dreams, and the joy, and the now. who are we if we don't refuse to be dead and gone? who are we if we don't refuse? to refuse is to carve a future we not even supposed to have. nothing can will a fertile thing to die. and let me tell you something, them dog dayz. them dying dayz are ova.

Climacteric Wonders

After James Baldwin's
"Staggerlee Wonders"

1

I always wonder what they think
the plantains are doing while they,

both thieves and ghosts haunt the space and land
these greens been ordained to grow on.

No, there is no church in the wild.
But nature has its laws to protect
the saints and what's more holy
than growing
despite the knife
or the rope lynching
the fruit of your labor?

> *Tropical America* // they erase.
> STOLEN LAND // we remember.

If the fruit don't
fall too far from the tree,
explain our diaspora.

> We everywhere.

2

i don't know a growing pain stronger than being both living and not human. if the earth swallowed me now, at least i know i'll die a real-ass g. know my ancestors will wait for me at the gates. know this body might arrive from a lab but this spirit been homegrown since before the boat. i. don't. give. a. fuck. how a colonizer feel. a colonizer ain't done shit for me but remind me why my homies can't breathe. why my mama got a pain in her back. why my anxiety flares at the siren. the trans-atlantic human trafficking. the displacement. jim crow. revisionist storytelling. 3 countries. still no land to call home. all we own is bullet holes and plastic cups we cannot recycle. the becky. the cops on speed dial. the fluoride in my tooth from all that project city water. the 4×4 apartment. the pigeons on watch. the drugs in the stairway. the homies growing up in and out of rikers. the babies waiting for they daddies to come home. the mamas waiting to breathe and take a day off when the daddies come home. the mamas who never get a day off when the daddies come home. the daddies who never get home. the daddies whose bodies make it home. the men who lose their spirit because the white man's prison beat it out of 'em. the homies who never get to come home to themselves. you feel me? so you see why sometimes, we just be dying to come home? how sometimes, that is the love story? black people make it home. the end? all i be trynna do is make it home. how sometimes, dying is the first and last time we get to make it home. maybe that's why we stay so ready to die. i don't know a lullaby more joyful than what the black body sings when it arrives home, unscathed. bruised but here. don't know a story more resilient than being black. both dead and alive. and i hope i survive to see the day, we don't have to die to make it home. all of us. to be black is to mourn every lynching, every broken heart, every time the sun is out and sky is pouring. i know somewhere a black mama is mourning. i don't know where she is but i am sure & i am

weary.

3

They do not ask me
if I am weary
for
they
do not care
to see what
T H E Y
have done to me.
T H E Y
take hostage everything yearning
yearn to hostage everything I am.
Everyone yearns to run away from them.
To rest and to sleep.

I wonder if they know how easily I become mush.
How soft this sun body can be.
How I am made of more water than soil.
How this existence means more to them than me.
How I am everything
without them and they are nothing
without the bomb, the chain and the whip.
What do they seek to be except all that I am?
Why can't they make some shit up and leave
my tired ass alone?
What do they cry about if not how they wished the sun
loved them like she adores me?
What is a weapon if not a cry for love?
What is a genocide if not revenge against God?
You think you can break something so impermeable?
You *tried it*

You cut my roots
and t h e y birthed
1,000 more.

4

I wonder how they think
    we green things made it,
      how we turned their dollar signs into culture.
      how come the cargo still here?
      how we sustenance for the poor?
      how we learned to save a life?
      to live as if our legacy was laughter.
      we sway with the wind of the storm
      water our leaves with the cry of the heavens
      drink mud with the children
and listen to their feet dance.

I, bitch who came from sugarcane and the falling of an empire,
know to grow from the root of my mama's tit.
Know to be ripe is to be ready for harvest or death.
Know to rest like it is my greatest accomplishment.
Know the machete will hurt but my blood will leave a stain.

For I, fruit or starch,
am ready to die
if it means to finally be free.

This Love, A Tragedy

there is a hypocrisy that shackles me
one that keeps me up at night.
it is as much my truth as it is my fear.
this tragedy, old and lonesome.
i want what does not want me.
america could be mine.
but what's the use in loving
such an ungrateful lover?

BLACK SPANISH

E' que hasta el español mio e' Negro
Y tiene un flow ratatata
Y no pide perdón, no se escusa ni se humilla.

My Spanish walks into a room
And you know it.
Leaves her *s*'s at home.

Vamo a lo que vinimo, she means it.
Her inflection a perico ripiao
If you know then you know

Nothing realer than some
Negras entrando al chat
Que se quiten o que recen.

Que ella vino a perrear.
We be twerking at the altar of our own rebirth.
Let that beat drop, our knees know exactly what to do.

E'te ritmo fue hecho pa' ella, aunque le nieguen entrada
La inspiración es ella. Las caderas todo ella.
Y dime que Negraaaa tan bella

E'te pelo, e'te flyyyy, e'ta percha.
Aunque copien, mientan, imiten.
E'ta chapa, e'te flow, e'ta mente
Igual Santa y Guerrera.

When you hear us
You got no choice but to see us.
We got accents by the pound
Que si Capitaleño, Cibaeño,
O me fui pa' Nuevayol.
In the Bronx hablan espanglish
Y lo tiran bien tira'o.
And here, no hay de otra que
Plantearse bien plantiao.
Nue'tro e'pañol no es malo
E' que nue'tro e'pañol es Negro
And you can't love our sauce and
not credit the cooks.
And myyyyy how that wrist be workin'.

This Spanish so Black you built a whole month
On our culture just to sketch us out.
This Black so Black it translates itself.
They got museums of our diamonds and gold.
Set up shop at the beach just to stare at our sun.
Accents thick as these thighs and as blessed as this Earth.
This for Negras around the world,
    We will no longer wait to be adored.
We built a Black universe and made ourselves the gods.

Eto e' Pa' Gailen, Pa' Sarah, Pa' Goyo, Pa' Maluca, Pa'
    Lorraine y Amara.
Pa' Dash, Pa' Jazmin, Pa' Jennifer, Pa' Cardi y la Bad
    Dominicana,
Pa' Marjua, Pa' Janel y Pa' Yaissa Pa' la Gata y Alida,
Pa' las Negras en los barrios y las mamis que nos crían.

Future Is A Space

let us learn to leave space for ourselves
in a future we can fathom. unperfect
and still here—we are not meant to be
robotic, just alive and green. we are simply
meant to grow. together. intertwine delicately
plow into me, respectfully. let our insides learn
the language of worms. let our unraveling be
holy & radiant. like the cosmos, we shine.
same dirt, different minds and imagined ideas.

what would you do if your identity crisis could
no longer be your personality trait? who would
you be if you believed you had answers before
you had anxiety? why would you keep playing
this race game if all they ever do is alienate you?
what is race if not a cloak of division invented
by the wilted and unwatered? who am i if not
some propagated plant clinging to the base
that is her faith? and i am not the inventor
or the champion. i am not the beggar or the bully.

i cannot heal a world in ruin. all i can do is water
the garden in me in us in the future of which we
belong. hydrated and calm, we trees sit idle
praying to the sky that the asteroid millions
of years in the making misses its shot to take us.
and if it does take us, *oh god, let it be.*

PART THREE

ON
BECOMING

Call Me By My New Name

opulently abundant or
thick with sap of sun-stained fruit or
money green and pregnant
call me mother of royal earth
call me cycle of ancestral survival
call me a cacti discovering church or
call me the *p* in *pressure* and *pollination* or
the eye in evolving and enticing
call me master of her own mind or
alive and dangerous
call me the beast that once and always was
call me that flame, that girl, that fertile flora or
call me by my new name
the biggest boldest vein on
the butt of a new leaf.

Between The Rut Of Us
Is Love

i feel it most / when we / unbraid and wash my type 4 hair /
peel mangoes with the razor of our teeth and bare brown
hands / pluck cucumbers from our five-acre garden / learn
how to grow *batatas* and *yucca* / hike up the side of the moun-
tain falconbridge abandoned after mining / pray in the form
of naps / ask god for more patience as we find our relationship
stuck in a moody rut / make a home of this rut and polish it
into a palace / forgive the rut of us for not knowing how to be
anything but a rut / uproot our insecurities / learn to love daily
/ learn to be present daily / ask love to stay for now / ask now
to be for as long as we need / make a baby / help that baby
grow / now we all blooming / cuddle in bed naked / listen to
rain wash over our thirsty tin roof / argue only to later laugh
over our egos' insignificance / cradle our marriage / write our-
selves onto the page / become an open book / cry into each
other / survive what does not become us but leaves us mis-
shapen / love what is messy but always enough

I Wanna Thank Me

I wanna admit that it took a pandemic to teach me to rest,
to fall into the fat that cushions my spine. Love me some *chichos*

There was a time when I did not like the extraness in my skin,
The flab that refuses muscle, rebukes BCAAs, spits out the *cines*

Them aminos that wanna make us into the same thing that wants
To break us. *Why would I wanna look like my oppressor?* Is the

Question—my body keeps crying. *I am meant to be thick and bold.*
Why should we disappear like they want us to? And I say, *you right.*

My bad, my fault, I thought this is what we wanted. We did not.
All we really want to do is lie and stretch into the skin of an
    uncured day.

There was a time when I thought the grief would consume me, but I fell
To my knees, my faith, let silence be the balm of ruddy mud &
    liquid eyes.

I danced with the gratitude and found my groove, and my groove found
My quilted collarbones, and *Diosa mía, thank you, because what a frame!*

This vessel, this beloved ecosystem, bottle green in the flesh. *It all
    becomes her*
Coil cloth woman, seeking to be full of all the cleansing blue water that
    keeps her.

Tropical Depression

The structure
of water is affected by our emotions.
Scientific studies have shown that water,
not only has memory but its structure
is affected by the emotions of people.
Abuela turns 95, her memory is fading
but she still remembers every emotion
the water inside her body carries. She says
the sad particles are starting to weigh her down.
She doesn't move her body much these days.
Afraid to spill
all her sadness back onto the world. *This pain,* she
smiles, is something
she's choosing to take with her. And I know she wishes the
generational trauma
will end with her. But Abuela has taught me everything I need
to know about surviving
depression. She says, *depression is a world unknown floating blindly in
the darkest parts of my mind.* She says, *I know how to swim but sometimes it
still feels like drowning.* To her, depression is a journey of silent suffering.
A celestial wave she says she will ride until she can hum it back to sleep.
That she can always weather the storm. Abuela says, depression was her
plus one at all three of her sons' funerals. Said, *I forgave depression when
he took your father away.* That she named my father Moses in the hopes that
he would be wise enough to part his way through this Red Sea of pain. I
tell her, *this world is trying to kill me and sometimes on my darkest days, I feel
like I should let it.* Abuela asks, *what do you do when you're depressed?* I say,

fill myself with the water I drink but can't keep from leaking. I say, *I am 7 on an island but suddenly I am the island and the salt water is all around me and I can't seem to escape it.* A gargoyle of earth snatched into dry land wishing for agua fresca, raising my white flag to the sky. And I still fight. Make this body a cyclone fronting all the blows life throws at it. This made putty with pressure, spirals back into seaweed. I am a greenling, evolving lungs into gills, turning water into oxygen, breathing depression back into dark seas. We can still feel the water rising over us. *But isn't it amazing*, Abuela says, *how much more ocean we are than dirt?* How much of this world we can swallow and not explode. How many burdens our souls can bear when we remember, we are not carrying them alone.

Heal With Me

Dear Mother,

This letter is meant to be a poem. And I am meant to be the words
on the page. Our blood is meant to be the ink at the tip of my pen. Our
countries, white paper full of disillusionment and grief. Our God may
be different but I know we pray the same. My birth is proof of your
glory. My strength is a root of your muscle. My journey is all because of
you as my gift.

Mother, I am your third and final becoming. I know they say three is
the number of completion. But I have spent this life trying to absolve my
displacement. First in Africa. Second, in the Caribbean. And third, here.
This country: my holy trinity. Mother, forgive me if I seem ungrateful
for your sacrifices. But I have not been happy here and I don't think you
have either.

I hold all of you deep in the core of my spirit and I ask you to release
our pain. I ask that you take a long walk with me. Remember that
young girl, still playing in your head. The one who dared so I could
dream. Mother, do you know that my greatest fear is dying for not being
brave enough to live? Do you know of this ache I carry? Do you know of
this history clenched between my tired teeth? Do you know how we
inherited this lockjaw? Why we communicate in screams. Do you know
how we became so angry? How my bones become sore from memories
lodged between blood marrow.

I know you wish to forget the storm, the rapes, the rivers of malice & machetes stained. I know you want to run away. I know you want to once again be that girl with high knees and small luggage. The girl who was not afraid to dive headfirst. I hope you see bits of her in me. I have not come up for air yet. I am still searching. Oh, Mother. How I wish I could show you what I see. How I wish I could help you find your mirror. How I wish I could take you back to dancing *palo*. I wish I could untame you. Wish you did not let them make your world so small. *Hay madre, hasta el plátano se cansa de ser marchitado, y no vuelvo a una identidad que me prefiere como esclava.*

Yours eternally,
Daughter of Diaspora

Mourning

All I know is somewhere
between the ages of four and five,
I started thinking in English.

All I know is my mother's accent
no longer rolled off my tongue.

All I know is I don't remember what
my father's words sound like in Spanish.

I still mourn all the other versions
that became of me.

Dance With Me

Dear Father,

This letter is meant to be a balm. To motion-freeze glittered specks of
your magic and love. My luster for life is because of your shadow. I have
learned to play with the ghosts of both our pasts. I do not wish to change
our fate but I do long for more time spent together earthside. You must
know I became obsessed with spirits in the hopes that I could teach
myself to be your clairvoyant daughter. Please understand, I am a writer
because there are things I cannot swallow and things I must uncover.

Father, I wish I had chosen to be a magician but instead I am a poet.
You have always been my realest thing. My biggest grief, your life and all
that did not come to fruition. I superimpose myself into what I believe to
be your world pleading my retinas to see or be seen. Are you with me?
Do you see me? I think of myself like some shooting star who is ready to
keep shining but loses its power along the way. Somewhere along the
way I got tired of being this gifted child you so loved.

A few times, I have been told they have seen you. Your shadow is
walking beside me. You are in the passenger seat, rolling down a
window. Los Adolescentes playing. Car rides made you feel the freest.
Dance with me and all the questions I wish to reconcile tonight. Do you
remember your birth? Do you remember mine? Gooey in our mothers'
sacs. The glint of light is a blinding mess, us tornadoing into existence.
The world in you, a black life that mattered enough for the universe to
birth you into existence even if only to burst you into flames.

I wonder if a shooting star can predict its own death? Don't answer that. One last question. Have you met God? Is she a Black woman? Does she look like your mother? Does she look like your mother's mother? Like life, giver of all things. When we buried you beneath her soil, did she welcome you home? Did she scold you about your drinking problem? Did she tell you how proud she is of what you grew to become despite how you let the world have too much of you? How you didn't leave much room for self-love. Let's take a moment and reconcile this love.

Yours eternally,
Daughter of Diaspora

How To Find Your Root

After Suzi Q. Smith's "How To Make Love"

The ancestors may be calling and you can't hear them, so you sway. Someone once told you, you have horrible rhythm and you stopped dancing. Your elders hummed and mourned. You went to karaoke and sang Celia Cruz and nobody clapped so you turned off your mic and bent inward. You dissolved your altar and throat and spat at the ground and chewed gum instead of mint leaves.

One day you realize your anxiety is asking you to search for God and you forgot how to look up. And the next day you want to trace your way back but you have become illiterate to nature and can't decode the leaves. And then you are walking home from work and your name is being called through the wind. And just before you lose your shit, you remember the recipe for tea Mamá gave you.

For heartbreak and other *pendejadas*. For those in need of grounding after leaving a toxic thing and other natural disasters. She tells you to find the freshest mint and citrus you can fathom. Peel as if it were ploy. The skin of a lime is sinister and sweet. Squeeze half of its acid into your pot. Mamá is not a woman who cries over men so instead she sings Rocío Jurado. She roams through her garden with her mini machete in search of the freshest tea leaves to sacrifice. You roam through Trader Joe's in search of your best alternative. In our mother's mother's garden we were once seeds. So it is so fitting that we turn to tea to make dust of our twisted trinkets and diluted dissonance. In this kitchen, you melt the mud of earth into medicine. You remember that love is never as sweet as honey. Honey isn't even as sweet as the poetry of honey. Poetry is a root.

And a root is meant to ground. To grind your expectations, your ill wishes, your dead ends. And so, this tea made of roots. This root of an orange leaf. The root inside of a lime. The root of the old you left behind. The one who knew not of the gold inside her teeth. The one who didn't chant or bow or praise. The idle you knew nothing of roots and left itself to rot. The root of the zest that guides you back. This root you become. Or you beget. Or at least here, you belong.

For Breonna Taylor

After Claude McKay's "If We Must Die"

ask me about peace
and i will tell you about sleep.
i will tell you about the nap that led me to my ancestors.
i will tell you that i want to die dreaming.
maybe like my grandmother, who after 2 countries,
several husbands, 6 kids, 3 cancers, and 95 years of
glorious living slowly rocked herself into an infinite sleep.

maybe we want to die choosing,
god willing, something more
than our hashtags.
if we're lucky,
maybe, we, all those born the color
of earth, will become more than just earth.

want to feel that bliss of a future freedom.
maybe we want some justice.
maybe we want more than the ringing in our ears
when our ancestors grieve of another lynching.
maybe we want more than the active exhaustion
of proving why we deserve to exist.

maybe we want to die and not be martyred.
not be a spirit the plague of whiteness gets to claim.
maybe we want to die sleeping.
maybe we want to sleep and not dream of dying.

here on the island, there is a drink for that.
morir soñando. i want the taste of that at my funeral
on the tip of my tongue. as i leave forever or for now.
if you ask me about peace, i will tell you of the day she
discovers black does not mean death.
but the complete absorption of light. and so she decides
if she must die, maybe it would be best to leave
like the sun. to one day, eventually, never rise again.

if she must die, can you let her soak
up enough light that she will go in peace?
if she must die, let it be in a dream
so illustrious she never wakes up.
let it be resting from the contracting of this worn body.
let her heart not beat with the panic of a bullet wound.
let it be still as the first day of may.
may her body be more than a thing to escape.

if she must die, give her a canopy
with hibiscus flowers at the bed of her feet.
soak her swollen hands in lavender oil.
let her knees and chest bend toward the soil,
let her mama hum her back inwards.
play her that lovely homecoming song.
if she must die, say her name.

Thank You, Toni

For writing me back to Earth.
I was nearly sea moss when
I read *Song of Solomon*.
I was close to withering when
I began *The Bluest Eye*.
I had lost my sense of self-worth
when *Love* fell into my lap.
I was becoming bitter fruit when
I finished *God Help the Child*.
Each story blossomed a new hope in me
that I too could be a world bender,
a rule breaker, a writer who writes her people
onto the page whether they have always
been the center is not up for debate or critique.
For we have always been our center. Our love. Our future.

My Body Cries To
Meg Thee Stallion

There is a sweet stream of sap coursing through my body.
    I know of insurrection like I know of this sticky song.
    The one the hot girls crack knees and necks for.
    The one that got Saartjie Baartman smirking in her grave.
    The one that made us forget they called us mules before calling
        us human.
    The one the horse sings when it retires the last bag of rice, a sweet
        mercy to see it fall.

Spent a decade earning its keep and finally get to shine.
    Fed the whole damn country town and now all she wants to do
    is dance
    no noose tied to her crown.
    Each bag weighing 100 pounds. Half of me split twice.
    I know more of baggage than i know of solid hooves
    and this body, always had a stage but never a spotlight.
    So here we are, hourglass front page. Jiggle worshipped.
    Time slapping beauty's déjà vu into shade. The tale of Africa
    & Texas in her arch. Skin a chestnut brown.

Watchu know 'bout that bone kind of Black?
Watchu know 'bout Southern kinks?
Watchu you know 'bout bodies that grow thick enough
    to sit they ass on yo' whole screen?
Watchu know 'bout a rap beat, tune of a freedom spell,
    & a stallion goddess singing the body a love song?

Watchu know 'bout waiting for summer just to feel the warmth of
   sun-kissed love?

A sweet stream of sap coursing through my body
I know more of femicide than i know of this safety
The one the hot girls crack knees and necks for.
Her body asking for peace & penance,
never truly knowing, what in the world
she is being punished for. . . .

Losing You

In another life, maybe I'd been more prepared for you
less afraid of ruin, more eager and willing, fashioning
armor with tender sack. Left to our own devices. Melting
pot of symbols for things that had not yet been birthed
into language.

You might've been not unlike what you are now, just as
complex and enlightened. Still searching and grasping.
Undaunted by life and death. More so, wanting to see it
all as is. Less attached to the particulars and more to the
servitude of finding yourself over and over and over again.
All the versions, a vessel, a world in you.

Looking onward past an existence that has not treated you
the best but served you a story. One that craves unending
and mending, shedding, layering, rebirthing.

You sleep so deep and easy and I wish you could see yourself
through my eyes in those moments. Soft warm putty
melting into mattress or chair, anyplace your body feels
weightless in. Your being, playing its own tune, noisy but
incredibly melodic.

I am quietest in these moments, hoping to decrypt those
sonic waves for things that will always remain unsaid.
Still, I lay there, hoping to hear you. My ears ask questions
that your voice will always mute and that is sometimes

enough. Knowing that something will always remain unspoken is some form of settled uncovering.

So I don't fight it. Choose to be more healer and less archaeologist. Try and put down my shovel, turn away the search party. Not excavate the versions of you kept buried for good reason. I decide on you, in that stillness, to not wake that part of you that wants to remain asleep here with me. If only, if for, this fleeting moment.

And I angle. Parallel to a frame I begin to feel one with. Willing to risk losing parts of me in this process. There is something so familiar the way my hips fit into yours. Carving space into a world that never welcomed bodies like ours to lay like this in the first place.

In that moment, I want to read you better than my favorite book. Study the outline of your frame. Shine angled to cheek. Light sweat on temple. Mouth half perched up, quiet yelling to the sky. Chest radiating with sun.

I swear you become a power plant. A solar panel.

It dawns on me that I wish to be more of you and less of me. Less needy of other. To exercise agency over my body and fully have it.

I am always colder. More literally and perhaps also in a distant sense. Body needing heating. Scary that it does not want to do it on its own. But also refusing to ask for help. I have not yet learned to speak. Scream. Loud enough for you to hear what it is I mean to say. Oh, how I wish to sound more primal and less defeated.

And you aren't always eager to howl at the moon. Sometimes, you wish to be the moon. And sometimes, I wish to be the tide. To see a part of you reflecting onto me.

In another life, maybe we took turns plucking anxiety and depression from ear to ear without ever having to speak. Without asking questions or demanding answers. Knowing each other's skin triggers better than our own. Leave wiggle room for each of us to become our own. Exchanging *I love you*'s for *I want to see you live your best life*. If not for anything other than because you are here, and you deserve it.

The Body, An Ode

ode to yogi pumpkin spice tea
& not a sight of a karen.
ode to the body without a trigger.
ode to the peace of hot deliverance.
ode to kimchi, kombucha & bone broth.
ode to indigenous peoples' takeback
of ancestral knowledge.
ode to freshly sliced lime, garlic,
ginger, red onion.
ode to cilantro for becoming my kale.
ode to the spirits' surrender.
ode to mangoes the size of my head,
that fall just ripe from my mama's tree.
ode to that juicy, earthy quench & resurrection.
ode to shrimad and 15-minute pranayamas.
ode to my belly for healing & unraveling itself.
ode to my brain for listening to its gut.
ode to my spirit when it hums my body back.
ode to the gastroenterologists giving tools not pills.
ode to the deep exhale of body in hammock.
ode to this body coming back
and back and running back
and crawling back and making it back,
                    home.

INEED$

I need money like I need therapy.
I need therapy like I need to survive white supremacy,
a pandemic, my mama, taxes, and climate change.

I need to survive like I need my ancestors
to feel even the slightest joy of seeing their offspring
do more than just work and die.

I need my ancestors like I need air.
I need air like I need a cliché to be as real
as the tired in my bones.

I need my bones to remember
how to rain dance,
how to money talk,
how to scam and spit,
how to slip and slide,
how to lavishly laugh
all the way to the atm.

She Be Doin' It & Doin' It
& Doin' It Well

Seli braids hair and gets rich men to buy her alcohol. They pay for trips to fancy beaches on long weekends. She be tanning her bum on the beach whilst converting her dollars to pesos in the hopes she can finally afford to finish her *abuelita's casa de campo*. What used to be a hut is now 4 acres of renovated dreams. A 2-car garage and 5 bedrooms for all of Seli's brothers and sisters, mom and grandma. She doesn't do much but what she does, she does it well.

•

Xiomayra sings to honor ancestors and get a bag. Both acts are an honoring of self. And the self likes trips to Rome on a white man's dime and jet. A tiny reparation. She has a beautiful creative mind but dem triple Ds are what pay the bills. And ain't no shame in it. There is a sort of redemption in Black excellence and luxurious joy. On a rolling basis, she sends her *dulce de leche papi* an invoice for the jet lag and quality time. History will remember that she made do and did abundantly well.

•

Yoki has never known anything other than *chapeo*. Her father introduced her to her first politician at 15 and ever since then she has had to learn to smile and give. *Chapeo* comes from the word *chapear*, which means to clear the land. One does not simply opt out of this kind of greedy world. One either hustles or gets hustled. She doesn't do much but what she does, she does it well.

•

Francina keeps her racks in her imported Telfar bags. She's got a red one that matches the Mercedes her new lover got her. They drive around the Malecón looking for good trouble and *teteo*. On Monday she's back to her white bag, paired well with laptop and lab coat. The women in her family are more than just leopard-print whips and seducing medusas. They sharpen their knife with a sponge. Which is to say, there are more quiet lethal ways to kill your prey than with the sweet slicing of a throat. A lick of cursed honey works just as well.

●

Live girls, big girls, hot girls, *chapis* with *chapas*, shorties in short-shorts and *mamis* made to milk their womanhood for all its worth. Serpents and *serenas* who said if they gotta live under this capitalist patriarchal colonial empire they gon' make it look sexy. Our kingdom is survival. Our communities turn centuries of fetishization into money. We do not judge or crucify women who were given no other choice and chose a bag. Chose to live. Chose themselves. And let God be our witness, we be doing it well and we do it for us.

Rent Free / Free Rent

i have officially lived in my uncle's house longer than he has. before me, it was vacant. before its empty walls, it was a mechanic's dream. before that, dust and dawn, a kaleidoscope of passports, whatsapp photo arrangements and monthly payments to a family friend who happened to work construction. before it was his dream, it was a gift of land my mother made to her brother. before the offering, it was scraps of savings from cleaning offices and wiping old folks' tired booties. between that and an accident that left my mother with fleeting arthritis, a strained neck and some g's to drop on land she has spent her whole life wanting to own. before she could own anything, she had to first grind herself to bones. before i could live here peacefully, i had to get through a stage of my life that almost killed me. so it may be that even living rent free will cost you everything.

A Day Like Today

After Rage Almighty's "Activist"

Today, I rise with the sudden ache of dawn.
My bones try not to remember the storm.
The whirlwind of trauma, try to shovel up my strength,
build myself a cocoon,
crawl back into my skin.

In 30 days all of me will be ash
and a brand-new me will emerge.
Isn't that kind of black-girl-glorious?
How we learn to heal the same way we learn to bleed.
Isn't that what God intended?
That the red seas seeping out of us be a picture of the
    impossible.
How we heal as much as the air we breathe,
as a testament to our stretch.
Have you never seen the canvas of our magic?
Show and prove the colorful rainbows that become of us,
we are no longer mourning,
not searching for grief,
not praying for freedom.

Today, I want to learn to play again
run wild with the wind,
lie in bright green grass and water myself into a flower.
Today, I choose to be a passion flower.
Isn't that all we fight for? To live a life worth living.

That our passions be a legacy lasting longer than our pain.
That the warmth of safety allow us to feel at ease
I have no space in my mind for grief in this place.
I am a movement of triumph, a singular army of joy.
I will not cry, not beg for God to numb me,
to erase the bodies that once were names.
I am a sharecropper teaching my garden
to develop the confidence of a vengeful queen.
To swallow this harvest and be full of power.
Isn't she just so enlightened, today?

What Nereyda, Ari, Jazmin, Gabbi & Keyshia Taught Me

Women like us are not special. We real. We all alike. Some variation of tint. Our kinks still bend the same. Our tongues, porcelain gold. We hold all that been forced on us between the opening of our pout and the crossing of our legs. Thick molasses, same consistency as blood. This swag be nectar. Be a priceless gem. A crooked crown or dented spoon, still we rejoice. You tell me we different kind of Black and I say, where? And how? What about this accent got me pedestaled and pit up against this "pick-me" wall?

My sisters from the Creole South put me on. Pulled me up. Called me Goddess, Queen, Worthy. Called me Black woman, no hyphen. Prayed for my safety. Texted me to confirm I made it home. I say yes. With them, I am always making it home. Always connected to women who let soul be their love language. No words. Just vibes. And the kind of sass I never want to grow out of. I am whole in this moment. Patra playing or Fefita la Grande playing, Tems playing or City Girls playing. Drinking something fruity and bound to make me bold. Make me drop it like it's hot. Test out these stallion legs. How fire this water swimming in our angled knees. How we prep our thighs for this ceremony. Age-old tradition in the meeting of our thighs. Ready to sweat next to a woman born on the other side of a Southern belt, in a country that tells us we are not the same and we are also not worthy.

Myyyy God, the way Nereyda, Ari, Jazmin, Gabbi and Keyshia: oceans apart move like they came from the same mama on the same night a man tells them: WHAT YOU MIXED WITH?

And they laugh. Everything. A whole universe and just as Black.

Let them do the lazy work of calling us rude bitches instead of digging up the cities of our inception kept silent. Call this our reparations. If we will never see redemption at least we have each other. Creole. Trigueña. Plantain Rich. Baddie from Texas. Miami. The Bronx. Harlem. Jamaica. Atlanta. Southern Belle. Sweet Lemonade. Cowfolk. Chicken feet stew. Gumbo with rice. Fufu with okra and fish that's fried. Sancocho con arroz. Avocado on the side. Scrapped this poor folk food and eat out of golden grills. We different to you. Yet all hold the same spice. We lounge in this skin. Bust it wide and open. Hips exhaling. Vibrating to the tune of a beat only we intuitively know. Got me feeling like life can't be this simple but y'all can't be this dense. Tell me, how do I divorce all the women in me who taught me about myself? And for what? For your token? Your box? Tell me a story you wrote where we don't end up as props, dead or in chains? Wish me well, you say. I laugh. WE. BEEN. DOING. THAT.

The Book Of Tina

In the beginning, there was Tina,
supreme Creole deity in true form:
a beauty therapist with gifted hands.

The type of miracle worker to sage
your spirit and lay down your edges.

Spritz hair sheen and rose water
all over this bloody place . . .

Mad sorcery enough to knock
a hater out without ever having laid a finger.

A classy bitch who some may have called
boujee and bold but she always knew God made
her first and the nonbelievers and skeptics last.

She drank from the fountain of youth, a muddy
juice for her to nourish light from and rise.
And myyyy did she rise.

Cracked open her rib and birthed the world with her.
Gave breath and rhythm to her flowers.

Told her flowers that they cute but way more
than just an earthy picking for others to pluck
and admire. Taught them to sway and hum. And sing.

God said *let there be light* and out popped Beyoncé.
God said *let there be rebellion* and out popped Solange.
God said *let there be R'n'B* and out popped Destiny's Child.

The epitome of Black-girl-magic. Watch how they churn
a miracle out of hot sauce and Southern gospel.

An Ode To Love

This is an ode to poems about men. This is also an ode to poems about women. A poem about me celebrating the men in my life who taught me you can be a man and feminist and you don't always gotta say it because sometimes what's understood don't need to be said. An ode to the women in my life who carry the traditions of their mothers interlaced between womb and gun. Whose fathers taught them to be sharp shooters and machete slingers. Whose mothers raised them to iron skirts and attitudes and never let tradition erase your self-dignity or desire for more out of life. The women who hold space for men to be vulnerable and broken. Who help them shed old skin, old bruises left unseen 'cause sometimes Black don't bruise as easily but hurt just as much. Women who don't excuse the rupture. Don't place blame on the bruised. Instead, look a little harder. Love a little deeper. Search for the battered blood vessels longing for kisses and rubs. This is an apology to the men I've hurt with my words. I'm sorry, I was mending myself and forgot to measure up a little more honey to cancel out the taste of lime. I haven't always been the best at baking pies. Sometimes I forget the main ingredients are patience and tender hands. This is an ode to my two older brothers who didn't blame me for being born with tender hands. Who allowed me to be without forcing gender norms on their baby sister. Who taught me to peep game and know a real one when I see one. An ode to the men who don't argue with us when we say *men are trash* and do double the work to shift the culture and prove us wrong. Who hold us, arms open, surrendering to all the toxic damage that has been done. Who cry with us. An ode to the love of my life who loves me on my worst day when I haven't been very loving to myself or him. Who forgives me even when he shouldn't. Even when he almost wants to give up. An ode to me also being the love of my life.

To allow myself to love without ownership or fear. An ode to love and cherishing every laugh, every smile, every dance. This is an ode to *Lemonade* and *4:44*. To every elevator that witnessed couples fight for their very existence to fight and love, privately within the confines of safety and growth and freedom and kept that shit a secret 'cause don't nobody need to be knowing our business. And leave it to nosey folk to try and ruin a good thing. Leave it to busybodies to try and interject their opinions on what God got planned for us. Tell them to watch what prayer and a good night's cuddle session can do for love. This poem is a testament to redemption. An ode to my grandparents who slept in separate rooms but still couldn't fathom living apart. An ode to being Black on both sides. To the clay that is this bond. How it hardens with the kiss of sun. This is an ode to all the children of the sun. Praying to find a love deeper than this hue. Beyond the scope of light. To penetrate through all this satellite. The fictitious layers that keep us away from truest selves. This is an ode to puppy love. To finding new synonyms for love with you. To you loving all sides of me. And to me loving all sides of you. To loving without ego and pressure. To letting things flow naturally. To the feminine and the masculine and the spectrum that is this kind of pretty and complicated and lively love. This is an ode to love.

What Do You Know
About Love?

I know love is like water. Bound to nothing and flowing
upon everything. We touch, we breathe, we are.

Sometimes a figment but mostly a hand, a hug, a dance, a laugh.
Love was in the room when she found a way to keep living.
Despite the hell that tried to break her.

And no, my love is not a white garden and a waltz.
It is not a glass slipper falling off at the end of a bland night.
Not a white knight or a blond boy on bended knee waiting for my fall.
My love does not tell me to give up my autonomy for its last name.

My love says I've been through enough.
Does not insist that I bleed to prove I deserve.

My love is not tied to a man whom I did not share a womb with.
Birthed itself. Do you not know how infinite this love is?
Do you know how many monsters hid from this love?

My love is an offering. You can share it with me,
but that don't mean it's yours. My love has traveled
with me for many years to choose you first.

She's both joyous and mad. Both tired and resilient.
Both sun and moon. My love is me choosing when
to stay and deciding when to leave.

My love has calloused hands she's proud of.
Can dismantle patriarchy, a broken ego, or
my anxiety with the warmth of these hands.

My love lets me color up all that I am.
Washes my hair and doesn't cringe at its kinks.
My love asks me if I've drank enough water today,
feeds me fruit plucked straight from a tree.

My love is a gentle man next to me with the fan on high.
It is too hot to even touch. So we nap while the sun
showers the day ablaze. My love tells me, my ancestors
did enough grinding for the rest of us. That it is okay
to rest. My love reminds me it is okay to be still.
To look up and revel at the miracle of life.
My love says through it all, we rise.

My love is a bronzed couple knocking coconuts off a tree,
is shea butter melting on melanin and skin.
Is a river after the rain has chosen not to stay.
My love still finds a way to pour.

A Love Letter To All
The Women Who Have Ever
Loved Him Before Me

In the first draft of this poem, I thought I could fix myself to insert some rich, fruitful motivational quote about how much better off he is without you. Some thug life shit like "you could never love him like I love him." I know that to be true. But I also know that sometimes, we humans get in the way of our own blessings. And I also know that life has a way of humbling you. So, this is me humbling myself to accept that I love him the way he loves me because of you. And love is only as good as the lover and the person brave enough to expend said love. And although I love him deeply in my own deep way, I'm sure you did too. And maybe still do. He wears your heart so well. His chest, a mosaic of all the women who have come before him, brave and selfless and wanting, hands cupping the remainder of themselves and willing to give it away to the man you one day hoped would give his love too. Brave enough to wander upon the unknown unguarded and hopeful. Having felt the storm and survived. With the strength and reassurance to keep going.

Secondly, I planned to brag about your man who is now my man but at the end of the day we both know is our man. Will always be our man. Even when you find yourself a new man. He is the kind of man women will always belong to. Not because of patriarchy. Or machismo. Or fragility. But because we want to. Because belonging to him is still belonging to ourselves and the part of ourselves we have because of him. Is belonging to a purpose. Deeper than the act of just belonging. The way we belong to this earth. The same way we belong to ourselves and those who gave us room to grow and belong somewhere else.

In the third part of this letter, I thought I'd tell you about his smile. Everyone who speaks of him describes him as a playful man. Lighthearted and goofy, his smile a sunshine. His laugh, a raw cackle. How we keep the inside jokes between the both of us. A funny intimacy between a chuckle kept secret. Padlocked between teeth and jaw. And mind and silly spirit. His gums finally getting to see daylight after a long day of being stiff and guarded. The sun melts into him, an offering posing as hot plasma keeps him gleaming. How he speaks sugarcane words, attempts to sweeten everyone's day. Forever offering up a joke in exchange for a laugh. Humor is his healing ritual. But you already knew that. You might've been the first to notice that laugh and make a home out of it. Helped birth its inception. Cradled his teeth between yours as his words gargled down your throat. When he cried in pain, in grief, in sorrow. You bird-fed his dreams back to him when he got tired of clenching them between his plucked wings. You might've coaxed him into a deep sleep on the days his insomnia made a monster out of the boy you loved. When he snarled in pain at what the world made of him, you let him bleed into you. You never panicked. And I'm grateful for you and the others for keeping him alive. For me. And his next lover.

DIY

I've been wearing a lot of skin lately.
Rubbing coconut oil in places I forgot existed.
Propping myself up and turning myself on.

I've been taking a lot of scantily clad sinful selfies lately.
Kind of photos got me feeling like a snack,
an appetizer, a meal and a dessert.

Tasteful nudes that don't belong in nobody's
DMs or no thirsty dude's phone.
They be like *Ayo ma, what that body do?*
Ummmm for one, not pop for you.
Not open herself up to be consumed and then returned.
Not allow any man to brag about having conquered it.

Not an object but a saucy Afro goddess worth praising.
How her hair bends and flows like Oshun.
White oleanders carefully place themselves on her crown.
How golden she looks after a warm bath. I can't help
but be exactly the woman my ancestors prayed for me to be.

To stride with a vengeance.
Sway my hips like I'm blessing you with my presence.
Because I am. And ain't it lovely?
How he begs to drink from this fountain.
How this holy water stay quenching his throat.
How he says a prayer and hopes to make it out alive.

The gloss in his lips when he comes up for air.
The way my skin does this thing
only mango-buttered skin can do.

How it melts at his touch.
I've been walking into rooms like the honey
that he's been searching for at the tea party lately.

The excitement has been in the wait.
So instead, I've been feeling myself deeply, lately.

Self-Portrait As A Green Goddess

for starters, this is a poem for the material gworls—the darlings who
     need a little
more than coffee to feel armed and fierce enough to face the day. it
     takes fashion.

some kind of colorful fur if it's cold out. some sort of fruity-patterned
     sundress
that tells the world: we ready to walk walk walk and strut because
     what choices

do we have? sit in the dark crying over x many horrors for what, honey?
     it costs
to shrink and it costs to grow so we might as well unlatch big-wide
     and flourish

just like a gworl with a shoot system and a root system and neither one
     of them
got time for underconfidence. there is a world that wants you dry and
     brittle so

rebuke the atheists and call yourself the goddess—green, gold, vibrant
     and edgy
be the woman, the god, the plant with the long vines and endless
     stretch. there

is no limit to your queendom, your hanging talent is bloodthirsty, you
     come in,
shake up the room. if they dare touch your leaves, they are never the
     same again.

I Say, "You Are Loved."

and my spine stops flinching.
and my arms unclench their fists.
and i cannot disassociate my heart from my brain.
and the weight of the world becomes a feather.
and suddenly i remember how to breathe.
and my body becomes an ode.
and my depression hums itself to sleep.
and my depression hums.
and i whisper goodbye.
and I can feel both my grandmamas' prayers.
and my brothers, I love you's, ring loud and clear.
and my mama had a dream and I listen to her gut.
and I remember that same divine energy pulsates within me.
and I step into my power.
and the water consumes me.
and I remember how to swim.
and I am running around in the rain.
and the sun is always dancing at my feet.
and palm trees sway with me and the breeze.
and I am always surrounded by water.
and I am always surrounded by love.
and suddenly I remember that I too,
am love and sun and green pastures and a beach.
and the water is also me.
and I am in love with the water.
and the water loves me back.

What Island Vibes Are Made Of

all i know is if the club don't got 4 horses,
10 scooters, 5 *motoconchos* and 7 *motores* parked outside—i don't want it.

if the dj don't play at least 3 different caribbean genres,
one for di waist, one for di feet and one for di soul—i don't want it.

if the dj don't ask where the single ladies at, and even the girlzzz
that came with they manz suddenly got attitude problemz—i don't
    want it.

if everybody not nostalgically slow bopping to the love kelly &
nelly shared while they were cheating on their boos—i don't want it.

if the fruity drink don't got real coconut milk mixed &
mingled with the ripest pineapple bits lips can fathom—i don't want it.

all i know is if the club don't got people sweatin' out they clothes
if love & sex don't infiltrate the dance floor & if no one is tempted
to leave barefoot and pregnant, then don't invite me, babes—i don't
    want it.

Amamantar

i did it for as long as my body would allow
each time a glorious sacrifice—anemia threatening
to rob us of this bond. nevertheless, we persisted.

four months later, my back gave out, my knees needed
our calcium returned to us, my depression creeped
up, slow and violent.

body feeding is hard. my therapist tells me i should
stop trying to find beautiful words to dress and dilute
the things that make me ache.

i ache for what was of this bond even if it tired me
out and over. *amamantar* is a ritual, a meditation,
a religious feast between two famished people.

when i hear the word in spanish, the first syllable
sounds like *amar*, which is love and to love
in arabic, *amar* means immortal and long life.

my doctor pats me in commemoration, so proud that
i have gifted my baby a little more life. the act of expelling
golden milk is seen as divine. she says, this bond is
as close to immortal as we will ever be.

I Am Rooting For You

After Lucille Clifton's "Blessing The Boats"

may that be enough to carry you through
earthside is a mess but so are we
still and in that stillness—enough
and   if it   /   we   isn't   then let us pray
that the knife is only used twice
one for the umbilical cord
and two for slicing dough not flesh—first
birthday cake to witness
olive gelatin dimples wait in glee
honey sweet brisket   a family   a crown of lit candles
enveloping your royalty   a gift
like the concept of water earth & sky

may you adore the elements in you
may you see the root of golden spirits
may the sacred kiss you each night
may you celebrate every breath
even the ones you don't remember
you were born   resisting
wishing   crawling   back into water
the water in me
an open palm and cross begging for our breath
the eternity of life   wise beyond age

may that be enough
may that resistance turn hopeful not hostile

may you inherit your freedom papers young
may that be the root of   why
you smile   coast cry cackle twirl a roar
i mean your birth is our surrender, our completion, our holy
i mean what else is a root to be   but a delicate
    free green thing
underground   swimming   right   on   through.

LIBRE

and though it may have cost
the weight of my body and bones

and though the summer drowned
me in patches of thick sap & sweat

and though i had to teach my hips
how to surfboardt anxiety to dust

and though waltzing to the tempo
of mangoes falling on tin roofs is shaky

and though i have never properly
played a *güira*, spoke their origin's tongue,
wept at their altar, or shook a mufasa into song.

and if all i have is these goose bumps,
smoke signals and butterflies whispering
bright green nothings of life as joy
at the crown of my temple.

and if freedom never comes,
i settle into rest as my sweet revenge
my hallelujah
my mercy
my hammock.

ACKNOWLEDGMENTS

I am infinitely grateful for my girlfriends; their poise and persistence to exist authentically inspires me daily and bore fruit to many of these poems. Thank you, Jazmin, Lorraine, Alida, Ari, Caro, Ruby, Minerva, Eva, Jenni, Faby, Esther, Zahira and Gailbriel, and to all the gworls around the world green and growing. Thank you to my agents, Erin Harris and Katherine Latshaw, for their positive and insightful energy. They advocated fiercely for my vision of this collection and I am so lucky to have them on my side. Thank you to my sweet editors, Pilar Garcia-Brown and Amber Oliver, for sifting through the mountains and mud with me. Thank you to the whole team at Tiny Reparations, Dutton, Penguin Random House and Folio Literary Management for doing this great and humbling work.

Many thanks to the beautiful and brilliant readers of the first drafts: Daniel O., Gisselle, Yaissa, Elise, Major, Frederic, Herby, Stacy, Elisabet, Jenny, Angelica, Liz and Melissa. You all helped sharpen my sword and strengthen my faith in the story of the plantains. Thank you to the poetry communities around the country who uplifted my poems, and for those who gave me a mic and a stage: Dallas Poetry Slam, Write About Now, Button Poetry and so many more.

To my mother, Aracelis, I am always in debt of your tenacity. Because of you, I thrive. To my father, Moises, I am so grateful to feel your presence still with me. The afterlife awaits us. To my bonus father, Leudis, thank you for being a tender ear and resource. To all my family and elders, thank you for your truth. To my grandmothers, Melania and Luisa, my strength is rooted in your fierce determination. To my ancestors, thank you for choosing me. With your guidance and love, I can soar. To my older brothers, Edwin and Daniel, thank you for reminding me to laugh after I cry. To my dearest partner, Alex, thank you for teaching me a million ways to fall in love with plantains.

Thank you to the island that has my heart and to the people split down the line by a river but have long built a bridge. Lastly, to my sweet *platanitos*, Rio and Hanler: I hope these poems one day bring you home to yourselves. *Somos Libre.* Thank you. *Gracias. Mèsi.*

ABOUT THE AUTHOR

Melania Luisa Marte is an American writer, poet, and musician from New York. Her viral poem "Afro-Latina" was featured by Instagram on their IGTV for National Poetry Month and has garnered over nine million views. Her work has also been featured by *Ain't I Latina?*, *AfroPunk*, *The Root*, *Teen Vogue*, Telemundo, Remezcla, *POPSUGAR*, and elsewhere. She currently lives with her partner and child between the Dominican Republic and Texas.

melanialuisa.com
♪ MelaTocaTierra
⊙ MelaTocaTierra